Alan Pianosmith came across Arthur in the mid 1980s at a recording trade show in Olympia, London. Arthur was standing in a queue to get in when an officious female asked him if he'd pre-registered. When Arthur told her that he hadn't she scowled at him and barked, "Name?"

"Professor Arthur C Throovest," came the reply. Officious woman didn't know whether to query this rejoinder or not. Her face was a picture. Alan held back stifled laughter and asked Arthur whether he'd like a coffee. It was the start of a long standing friendship and working relationship… Alan would record all of Arthur's songs for him.

It has seemed that the pair have known each other all their lives. In a sense they probably have. This biography has been highly condensed to embrace only significant millstones in the professor's life. Millstones that we've all carried from time to time.

Enjoy.

FAME, FORTUNE, POPULARITY... HOW I AVOIDED THEM ALL

Professor Arthur C Throovest - an autopsy – a novel – a novel autopsy?

OK then... a biography

Alan Pianosmith

Places, events, times, dates, names, liaisons, currency and chronology have been changed to protect the guilty as well as the innocent. The only thing remaining unchanged is the underwear.

Copyright - © *Alan Pianosmith*

The Throovest Foundation

BEGINNINGS

Although born in West Bromwich, Arthur lived out his formative years in King Edward Road, Moseley, Birmingham. It was post-war Brum. Rationing. Arguing neighbours. An occasional suicide. Just three car owners in a cul-de-sac of some 160 souls. No cash. Kicking tin cans in the road. Breaking windows & blaming someone else. Saturday morning cinema. Saturday afternoon bussing into Birmingham - on his own, aged six. Kings Heath Infant & Junior schools. His mother sent him there because she didn't like the condition of the outside lavatories at Moseley Junior School. Thick fogs. Thick snow. Thick stews. Thick people... mostly.
The week was punctuated by trips to Woodroffe's Music Emporium in John Bright Street for accordion lessons. By age seven, Arthur knew all there was to know about chords. The bass buttons on a squeeze box spelled them out in logical lines. This knowledge would become invaluable. A happyish time when he just did what was asked of him.

He scraped through the contentious 11+ exam, moved on to Moseley Grammar School where he didn't get 'O' levels in maths, physics, Latin, geography, woodwork or biology. He didn't excel with other subjects either, but he did have a band - or 'group' as such ensembles were then dubbed. 'Throovest's Performing Squirrels' were more an enigma. A puzzle, rather than a coherent musical outfit. Many thought that Arthur's rather disjointed and avant-garde approach to popular songs and life in general must surely have influenced fellow Moseleian, Jasper Carrott and, latterly, Lord Taylor of Warwick. Or was it the other way round?

Leonard Lanyard was also at Moseley but four years ahead of Arthur. Leonard also had a band but it would have nothing to do with Arthur's lot. Four years apart at school is the equivalent of a billion light years.

"Can Arthur join our group?" asked Leonard, now with his own professional band, the Merrye Men. School was now a distant memory to both of them. Leonard had simply turned up on Arthur's doorstep. Arthur was out.

"Of course," said his mother.

Arthur was immediately and irrevocably shot into oblivion by his mom without any personal input, action, prior knowledge or consent. A trait and pattern that was to follow him for the days of his rest.

Well, there were no 'phones back then... much, so you just had to 'call round' if you wanted to speak to someone. Mobiles? Mobiles were things that hung over babies' cots. Mother knew Arthur would readily consent to this offer. He was sick of Birmingham, working as an ice cream salesman from a left hand drive Ford Anglia van. He earned so little that he ate the cones and wafers into which vanilla ice cream should be shoved. To Arthur this was expedient. Necessary. Breakfast. Lunch. Walls Ice Cream Limited docked every cornet and wafer he consumed from his meagre wage. It didn't bother him. It was normal business practice back then in 1964.

The Merrye Men were signed to a London manager, Larry Varnish. They were about to take Germany by moderate drizzle, but not before Arthur was to go on a long, planned holiday. Since there was no fixed date for the German gig, it seemed OK for him to go on a pre-arranged holiday to Sweden with his oldest school friend, Ricardo Palomino. (Ric's family bred horses). They thought Palomino was a great name in the equine world and the emerging world of PR, too. Their real name was Zocko. Not retaining their real name was a mistake. Search engines today would always find any one of Ric's relatives under 'Zocko'. Palomino throws up some 27,000,000 websites.

SWEDEN BY STORM

The pair sailed from Harwich on a violent sea. Arthur was so sick, he didn't get out of bed for 2 days, except to attempt to play Beatles' songs on the deck. Ric would drag him out, hang the first engineer's guitar round his neck and brag to a bunch of Swedish girl students that Arthur was about to hit the big time. The ploy to impress didn't work too well, however. After but a few bars of 'Love Me Do' Arthur dashed to the rail, simultaneously dashing Ric's hopes of making good with the stunning female Swedes as he gently heaved-ho to the not-so-gentle heaving-ho of the ship. Dry land couldn't come too soon.

After two days in Gothenburg Ric's sister took the call. Everyone had a 'phone in Sweden. "Arthur must get to Cologne immediately. The band has a month's contract at The Storyville Club."

Without thought or return of call, Ric and his sister waved Arthur off from the north of Denmark as he trundled away in a rattling old WW2 steam train; the overnight to Köln via Hamburg. Surely the life of the young Throovest was going to take off. Soar. Encounter new meaning. Imbue fame and fortune.

Nope.

At the age of 17, Arthur was still at ease just doing what people asked of him. He never queried anything. The fact that he was about to play a four hour set with a band he didn't know, playing music he was only vaguely familiar with to an audience who wouldn't understand him. His knowledge of the electronic organ being marginally greater than nil, didn't faze him in the slightest. Somehow it would all work.

And it did… Sort of.

KULTUR SHOCK

The Merrye Men were billeted in a flat owned and shared by a Yugoslav maniac, one Johnny Jovanovitch and his large, violent, German wife. The taps had been removed from the bath and there were no facilities to even make a cup of coffee. The band played their first night at the Storyville. They returned in the early hours, fell into Werner's Bar in the basement of the block of flats and sipped Bitburger, schnapps and Pernod. Werner warmed to the band immediately and put the Merrye Men's newly released single on his juke box. The record was never going to make the group famous but in 1964 anyone who had made a record was considered fab and gear. It was also on an independent label – Solar. Leonard would often repeat the name and fall about in guffaws of mirth. "So-lar, So-lar", he would sing, as if mimicking a radio ad. "So-lar, So-lar-sole ar-sole ar-sole". Somehow the rude joke tickled him so that he cried with laughter. He explained the gag to Werner in his very passable, up and coming German. Werner laughed too, but his face betrayed either a complete lack of understanding of the joke or, more likely, making fun of your record label was probably not considered to be the German way.

The band was exposed to the realities of post-war hedonism in a Köln that was trying to redefine itself. A reality which was both incomprehensible, shocking and totally beyond their Brummy naîvety. Two couples just came into the bar, got their drinks and started to unleash their passion. The two men with each other and the women together enjoying a snog. The band just thought it best to talk about the Beatles' latest single and what the weather might be doing the following day.

Eventually, the band crawled into their respective bunks up on the 14th floor. No sooner had much needed slumber overtaken them when screaming and shouting could be heard up and down the otherwise deserted Strasse. Mrs. Fat German was hot on the heels of maniac Yugoslav, brandishing a large bread knife, which glistened in the street lights. This was a regular event and the band simply slept through ensuing fracases. They also learned to sleep through the gentle tones of cars crashing over the tramlines. The long, straight cobbled main road divided right outside the flats. The tramlines, however, went straight on. Hence, inebriated Kölnischer revellers simply followed the tramlines and did an MG34 machine gun impression as they du.. du..du..du..du'd over the ancient, dilapidated sleepers. This was followed by what the band considered to be swearing. As the days and weeks unfolded they learned that the very loud, early morning stream of semi-intelligible German vocabulary was, indeed, swearing.

There was also the strange paradox of the demonic Mrs. Fat German mercilessly thrashing Arthur till he found refuge by crawling under his bed. This was for a serious misdemeanour… he was wearing jeans on a Sunday. Life was, indeed, surreal at the Jovanovitch's.

It was a blissful time, however and, mercifully, all very innocent, corporal punishment apart. It was clear that previous bands appearing at the Storyville were intent on sex and drugs as well as the rock 'n' roll. Girls would roll up after the show, making it abundantly obvious that they wanted more than autographs. The Merrye Men only ever gave them rock 'n' roll, however, which mystified the groupies. A beautiful blond girl latched herself onto the Fewzy's equally handsome lead guitarist. Piers had a fiancée back in Solihull, so this looked like it might be tricky. Somehow this Teutonic bombshell cadged a lift back to her flat in the group's van. Piers politely escorted her to the front door. There was a short dialogue, he shook her hand and she disappeared into the vestibule with a look of consternation and disbelief on her fabulously gorgeous face. Not even a peck on the cheek. Integrity. Arthur learned volumes about integrity that night while the rest of the band ribbed him, laughed at him and suggested there was something wrong with him. Piers ignored it all with great dignity. His fiancée would be assured of a great future husband.

Soon the band was back in Blighty. What next? A loaded question to which none of the members of this slightly old fashioned five-piece group had any answers. Larry Varnish had the answer, though. "I'm putting a girl singer with you." The notion was that 'Loretta Lanyard' would make it easier to sell the band - especially back in Germany. The ploy obviously worked because the Merrye Men found themselves bumping down the ferry ramp and driving across Belgium and up to the outskirts of Hamburg. It was dark, cold and snowing heavily.

SIX PIECE - AND BACK TO DEUTSCHLAND

Loretta, (Lettice McGivelry) was easy going, paid no attention to the drummer's advances and didn't quibble over her stage name. Leonard was not so pleased. Although the girl was attractive, dubbing her with the same surname implied that she was either his wife or sister. The punters always thought of her as his sister which irked Leonard no end. He inferred that people didn't think he was a match for the delectable Loretta. Or, worse, that he was a queer.

The North German tour was a long one. It was January, bitterly cold and each engagement was for a week in each town.
The venues were all converted cinemas and the billeting was always in the old projection rooms. Hence, it was dark, freezing, cramped and was not ideal for Lettice. The lads were very accommodating, though. They would make sure she had her privacy. There was no conflict over bathroom arrangements.

There was no bathroom.

The cinemas were always next to the rail station so there was this bizarre scenario whereby bemused Germans would witness strange, long haired Brits filing out of a tiny side door and into the Hauptbahnhof bog in various stages of undress. Lettice would borrow the lads' coats and vanish into the 'Damen' under the suspicious gaze of the ubiquitous polizei. They never challenged her. Either they thought she was one of their own 'bag' women or, more likely, they knew exactly what the score was. After all, the popular British bands were a permanent feature of post war Germany and the inadequate living conditions were well known by the locals.

The band was playing 5 hours a night, every night. Loretta Lanyard sang for about a third of that time and the new format and repertoire was working well. A week soon passed and on they went to the next gig. Finding the venues proved the easiest part - just head for the rail station and the tanz palast (dance palace) was always next door. For some reason the Germans built their picture houses next to stations. Maybe trains ran so late that travellers would need to while away the time; das Lichtspielhaus adjacent filled the bill. The whole dance hall chain was owned and run by Manccetta Bulivari. He was one of those guys you didn't ask too many questions about. Instinctively, you knew he was a crook. A big crook. He had an 'arrangement' with the polizei and that was something else you didn't ask about.

After weeks of living out of dark hovels, Leonard was called to the box office-cum-club lobby where the 'phone was. It was Larry. He'd fixed the band to do a month's residency right up near the Danish border. It sounded really fab. And gear. So, instead of driving back home, the packed J2 van lumbered up the autobahn to Schleswig Holstein.

NORTH GERMAN PARADISE

The Schleihalle was pure luxury. Unadulterated bliss. No bath, but a room with a sink, hot water and a lavatory. The weather was minus 15 degrees celsius and the sea was freezing over. But it didn't matter. The Schleihalle was blissfully warm and Arthur relaxed and laughed with the guys and gal at such a turn up for the books. The band couldn't believe the total change in circumstances. The beer was cheap for the band as well as for the staff, all meals were included, the clientele was polite, refined and very appreciative. Lettice was loved to bits and she made many new friends who couldn't do enough for her. The whole band was invited out to tea regularly and Arthur was greeted by name in the strasse. Life was sweet. Money was plentiful. The music was improving and Arthur embarked on the wacky side of his nature.

The Schleihalle used ultra violet lighting and during the guitar solo in 'Hootchie Cootchie Man' Arthur took 2 white hankies and did a mock Morris dance. All you could see were 2 white prescribed circles, orbs and ellipses as he swished and swirled in 6/8 time. Leonard laughed like a drain, but the audience took it all very seriously. Leonard saw the mood and, over the mike, he gave his version of the history of the Morris Men of Olde England in a deadpan, lecturial style... and in fluent German. Arthur had wished that this oratory could have been filmed. The Merrye Men's front man was utterly convincing and after the show many punters came up to ask him - and Arthur - more about this strange English folk dance. Leonard embellished the Morrismen story until Arthur thought plausibility must surely run out. But the German nature has that innate ability to trust anyone who feeds them a line with a straight face. Remember Hitler?

Leonard also had the incredible ability to translate songs into German on the hoof. Although it was February, the band played 'White Christmas' because it was snowing heavily. Len translated as the lads busked their way along. The interpretation was so good that he got a standing ovation.

The gig lasted 3 months. During that time Arthur had his passport stolen by the wife of the drummer of a local band that played downstairs in the Schleihalle. He was East German and they were desperate to get the family over to the West. Arthur was easy pickings. Asked to leave his coat in the bedroom while the band 'enjoyed' tea, Mrs. Nasty Woman sneaked in, stole the passport and waved the band goodbye, the Stanley Knife already in her hand to cut and switch photos. You could do that then and get away with it before the days of holograms, UV detection and chips.

Arthur often mused about the episode, which he never reported as a theft. Why didn't she just ask him for the wretched thing? He would have had to visit the Consulate in Hamburg whether the passport was lost, missing *or* stolen. What would it have mattered?

Hey ho. Maybe the very inconvenient misdemeanour helped somebody over the wall. Either way, Arthur would never know. Youthful innocence. Stupidity. Immaturity. Loads of things that you simply don't know about until you grow up. With Arthur, growing up took a long, long time.

Schleswig was good. There was even a brief holiday when Arthur escaped to the island of Amrum to visit 2 chamber maids who worked there. (They had been customers at the Schliehalle). Anthrax, the drummer, came with him and they both wallowed in free time, beautiful innocent female company and an introduction to Asbach, the famous brandy from Rudesheim. Asbach would feature again in Arthur's life… but not for another 45 years.

But the carnival was over. The long drive back to Ostend was a real downer. Larry hadn't come up with another life saver. Clearly Lettice wanted to move on. The guitarist was going to marry and settle down and Arthur was still going to do whatever was asked of him. It would be a long Summer.

BACK TO BLIGHTY

Back home, it was as if Arthur had visited Mars in a time machine. Landing back in Moseley Village was as if time had stood still. Or maybe just shuffled about a bit. His old friends bombarded him with interminable questions about his exploits. Nobody had ever been abroad. They didn't even know what or where Germany was. The only thing Arthur's mates knew was that Hitler was probably dead and they were all foreigners over there and that the war involving that country had knocked their families about a bit. In some cases, a lot. And that the Beatles had worked there. Arthur embellished the inherently exciting stories and splashed huge German cigars about as if they were Park Drive nub-ends, much to the delight of most of the Gigi coffee bar's customers. Arthur took great delight in dramatising the outrageous behaviour of his Cologne landlord and landlady. His mates simply didn't believe him. More plausible was the operation of the Storyville Club. The bouncer carried a gun and the head waiter resembled Dustin Hoffman's 'Ratso' Rizzo in Midnight Cowboy. This slightly deformed relic from the war shuffled quickly from bar, storeroom and shot glasses. Arthur explained to his chums how 'Ratso' would stack a huge tray with about 100 schnapps glasses and fill them by continuously pouring cheap schnapps from a great height. The technique was the same as that of the Woolworths cafeteria tea pourer in the 1950s. High Tea had a totally different meaning in Woolies by Birmingham's Bull Ring. In the Storyville, it was compulsory to have a schnapps with your beer. No option.

ENTERTAINERS, RED JACKETS & VANCE

An advert in the Birmingham Mail struck him. 'Musicians wanted to form a band to perform pop and dance music.' Such a band had never existed. A challenge, surely. Arthur was the only one with any real experience among those that turned up for the audition. The idea was the brainchild of a Black Country engineer, one Vance Blanchard, who was successful in running trad bands on the side. It was a good idea. Once the candidates had been paired down to some guys who could actually play something, Vance arranged for parts to be written out and the boys assembled for the first rehearsal.

The parts had been written by a seasoned pro dance band orchestrator. Mercifully, Arthur's training on the accordion came to the fore. He was the only one who could read the parts with any degree of fluency. Patiently he routined sax, guitar and drums through such standards as Tea For Two, Whispering and Fly Me To The Moon. The guys already knew the top ten of the day. Tie A Yellow Ribbon and March Of The Mods were thrown together in no time.

It turned out that the band was a tax loss initiative for Vance. He spent money on the new venture to offset taxes on the fortune he was making running jazz clubs. You could make money then in the mid 1960s. So, red jackets were ordered, publicity photos taken and the band's name plastered everywhere. It was Arthur who came up with the masthead 'The Entertainers.' It was a good brand. The outfit **was** entertaining. It was unusual to see a band smartly and brightly turned out, well rehearsed and with a repertoire that spanned the dance band / ballroom standards together with an amalgam of top ten tunes. The Entertainers could switch from a waltz like 'Ramona' to the Beatles' 'I Saw Her Standing There' or Tom Jones' 'Delilah' effortlessly and convincingly. The enterprise worked. Arthur had simply gone along with another idea. It was working. But although popular, it didn't propagate fame nor fortune. He got a daytime job again.

Brewers, Birmingham, was the job in a succession of jobs. It involved cutting and despatching upholstery material. The two elderly owners rather liked Arthur even though a lot of the 'phone calls to the firm were for him. Invariably it was Vance wanting to discuss gigs with the Entertainers and matters arising. Arthur was the assumed leader of the band. Although Messrs. Brewers feigned irritation at the calls, they didn't really mind. It brought a bit of life to the otherwise dull business of cutting up cloth and packing it for delivery. In any case, Arthur was a good and reliable worker. The manager interrupted a particularly busy day. "Let me check your work, Arthur." He announced in front of all the other staff. Cloth was measured using a yardstick which you placed over the running edge of the cloth. The technique was to shunt the material along passing from one hand to the other, the yardstick marking off each shunt using the thumb as a kind of buffer. The very long order was duly checked in front of the slightly nervous gaze of the workforce. How far out would Arthur's measuring be? To the amazement of everyone… to the astonishment of Arthur almost 40 yards of cloth was found to be exact to the inch. "Well done, Arthur," said the manager. "Any complaints we get from your work will have me tell 'em where to shove their moquette." It was common for upholsterers to beef about being short measured.

Other jobs followed. Driving for Gothic Electrical was one. Arthur enjoyed plowing up and down the West Midlands in a 30 cwt van. It was a freedom of sorts and he was left to get on with it. The end came when the manager responsible for the fleet of vans loaded Arthur's wagon with electric motors destined for a factory in Telford. Although the consignment didn't take up much volume, the weight was deceptive. The van hit a pothole just outside Wolverhampton. Bang! The whole of the vehicle's suspension collapsed. Arthur was ordered into the boss's office and given a dressing down. Arthur had only been doing what he was asked to do, after all. It became clear that there was a collusion between boss and manager. There was no way that manager man was going to share any of the blame, let alone admit it was entirely his fault. "You might like to offer my job to another more splendid fellow," suggested Arthur. Well, he didn't exactly use that turn of phrase. Some words drew on an authentic translation of the vocabulary of the Cologne tram rails revellers.

The Entertainers gained a degree of popularity… in Birmingham and the Black Country at least. But it was never enough to live on and it was clearly always going to be a semi-pro outfit. No matter. Arthur could meld his piano playing ability to retail sales and work for Cranes Music. And so he did.

Pianos and organs were very big business in the 1960s. He had the gift of making an old knacker of a jangle box joanna sound like a Steinway. The gifting didn't go down too well with the rest of the staff, however. Arthur was selling pianos and organs like they were Sparky's original magic machines. Sadly, the magic would soon fade and no longer be fashionable. Every effort was made to displace him - together with his popularity with the punters. A brusque Scottish manager, Johanne Lard, knew the perfect vehicle to bring about the successful Mr. Throovest's departure. Hit him in the pocket. Wages were delivered in cash via small, brown envelopes. This particular Saturday the wage slip tally didn't corroborate the cash inclusion. When asked about the significant discrepancy, the dour Mr. Lard accused Arthur of selling merchandise under the ticket price. Arthur never gave discounts. He never needed to, whereas the other salesmen always shaved prices in a desperate attempt to clinch sales. This fact and unjust anomaly was pointed out to Johanne. Johanne pointed to the door. Arthur exited by the door only to return the following week to attend an in-house tribunal chaired by Cranes' MD. Again, the collusion between boss and manager was obvious and the outcome prophetic. This time Arthur pointed to the door himself, followed his own directive and never came back.

SUPERSALESMAN AND COMPLETE WRECK

It was at a time when Yamaha organs were introduced into the UK. Ryland Skucheck had snapped up the whole of the West Midlands as franchisee for these cheap and novel instruments. Ryland immediately gave Arthur the manager's job at his shop in Coventry. Mrs. Skucheck thought she'd won the pools - every week. Arthur would drive down to the HQ in Sheldon, slap a briefcase on the office counter and pull out great wads of banknotes and copy invoices. It was 'Arthur C Throovest, Sales Director' within a few short weeks.

A massive piano and organ emporium opened in Birmingham City Centre and Arthur was in charge of all of it. Ryland bought up all the competition and in no time Arthur was the boss over 9 shops and some 30 plus staff. The flashy car, smart suits and generous director's emoluments went to his head somewhat and, like an idiot, he carried on playing a professional gig backing cabaret in a small, city centre restaurant until the early hours of the morning... 7 days a week. It nearly killed him. He ended up with ill heath, quitting his job and wondering what on earth to do next.

Although unfit, he auditioned for another cabaret-backing job in Jersey. No problem. He drove down to Plymouth in a wreck of a Thames van. The van's unserviceable condition matched Arthur's unserviceable condition exactly. The overnight sailing dropped him off at 6.30 am in St. Helier and he went straight on to rehearse the acts and nearly collapsed with stomach pains. A drunken Scottish doctor in Jersey's only hospital said "Ulcerrrrs, mate," and walked out of the examination cubicle leaving Arthur the conundrum of what he could or should do. He drove to the ferry and sailed home.

A good friend from his teenage years, Jethro Hollins, heard of Arthur's plight and immediately got him to work for his tiny engineering company on the outskirts of Brum. Arthur had no idea about the machinery - they were devices for applying adhesives. Although he knew nothing, it was a relief to have a friend on his side who was sympathetic, supported him knowing he wasn't well and had a wonderfully cavalier attitude to life. Arthur drove round Britain representing Jethro's mini enterprise and found himself in front of the good and the great who needed stuff gluing together.

It seemed that the whole world was being stuck together. New, hybrid adhesives were the trendy, modern alternatives to welding, pop riveting and bolting. Mr. Throovest became a popular visitor to some of the greatest brands in the world. He had a knack of finding different ways to assemble components and chief design engineers adopted many of his ideas. In the adopting, Jethro's glue machines were selling well. Arthur found it a bit disconcerting. Airbus wings were held together using an air-driven glue mixer that had been put together by an ex-bricklayer. Plessey was pouring Araldite epoxy into tiny potentiometers and British Aerospace settled on Jethro's glue mixer to stop night sights from coming apart in a war situation. Even the new Mini Metro was held together by sticky stuff and the MOD glued its 35mm ammunition with a top secret, colourless liquid.

This strange and curious industry introduced polyethylene foam to Arthur's creative nature. It was a brand new material. Tough, completely impervious to water and very easily cut and welded. Within no time, the first four man canoe had been created using Karl Freudenberg's wonderful foam invention. Jethro loved it and soon the robust, lightweight dart of a skiff was poised at the start of the River Severn Raft Race. It looked odd. A bit like a blue, 40 foot-long sausage. The Bewdley Rowing Club howled with laughter at the notion that such a craft could float, let alone move through water. They stopped laughing, however, when 'Quadrulius' glided over the finish line a good twelve minutes ahead of the Rowing Club team. They hated Arthur. The local hospital loved him though. The highly mobile and manoeuvrable canoe got loads of publicity, attracting additional donations to the infirmary - the sole beneficiary of this annual fund raising event. Future designs by Arthur also won the race for three consecutive years. The mood had changed. Folk were no longer going to enter the raft race if the successful 'Professor' Throovest was taking part. 'Professor' was now the title taken up by the media. Arthur talked to the organisers. He suggested building a Robinson Crusoe-type raft that broke all the rules. The organisers would then officially disqualify him before the race and the craft would gently float down to Bewdley to the strains of pop songs of the day, played by Arthur on a piano bolted to the deck. The dozen or so friends who crewed the vessel all wore evening dress from the waist up, swimming trunks from the waist down. The team became more popular than ever and the revenue doubled for the hospital. It went to national TV. Bewdley Rowing Club went crimson with rage.

It was time now, though, to slip into something more comfortable. More familiar. Something that would be fulfilling. Music must surely be the way forward. Cyril Kramer was the very man to come up with the goods. Rather like with Jethro, Cyril was in just the right place at the right time. "I need help recording stuff," said Cyril, "Come and work with me." And so the creative side of Arthur was glued - sorry, added -   to the wacky bit and the tie-up with Cyril was going to last for the rest of his life, on and off. The amalgam was perfect. Arthur played keyboard and in the early days helped bands and singer / songwriters to make half decent albums. All on cassette tape in those days.

He and Cyril were to make literally hundreds of albums for wanna-bees and it was a happy time. Frequent trips involved trade shows in London and these eventually precipitated an annual visit to the Music Trade Fair in Frankfurt.

DANCE BANDS AND CABARET

The recording venture also got him back into playing piano. The old Entertainers band had reformed and tracked Arthur down. They'd secured a valuable residency at the George Hotel in Solihull. It was a perfect situation just round the corner from his maisonette, a regular Saturday night dance and some 200 gigs a year playing for dinner dances throughout a long season. The mix of ballroom dance material and top 10 pops was by now an established format and the whole scene was immensely enjoyable for everyone. The money was good too.

The venue was also HQ for the Masonic Lodge for the district, so all the very many Lodge dinners were always held there and the band was thrown in as part of the deal. It took some getting used to, however. Each Masonic dinner had its own formal and traditional setting - Ladies' Nights, Worshipful Master's dinners, welcoming of new 'brothers' and so it went on. Playing for these dinners was an art in itself. The band could be but a few bars into a tune when a gavel would smash down on the table, followed by another 2 gavels from different points in the dining room. "The Worshipful Master will now take wine with the ladies," bellowed the MC. Everything stopped while glasses were raised and the toast was toasted. A few minutes later, "The ladies would like to take wine with the Senior Warden." Then there was the Treasurer's toast, The Deacon, The Stewards, the Tiler, the Chaplain, the Marshal, the Deputy Grand Master... It seemed to go on forever. It was a wonder that the band ever got to play a tune all the way through. It wasn't a wonder, however, that assembled company ended up sloshed. Even at a sip of wine per toast, the alcohol consumption was rather on the high side. Nonetheless, the money was good and the work regular. Since dosh from recording with Cyril wasn't exactly brilliant, the gig was a necessary earner for Arthur.

He was never quite sure how Kevin Alibone had found him. Kevin just turned up at the George one night during a Masonic dinner and button-holed him. "Got a great job backing cabaret, Arthur. It's yours if you want it." The offer was tempting. Although it was in Stratford, the job sounded much more interesting than repetitious, drunken punctuated dinner dances. The promise of backing some top acts was too much to resist. Arthur joined bass player Kevin and a drummer the following Thursday for a band call at the Toll House, Stratford Upon Avon.

The turns were all top notch. First up were Los Salerosos, a pucker flamenco duo. Arthur felt the blood drain from his head as he cast his dilating pupils over their scores. The music looked like a 32 legged spider had performed a Spanish dance over parchment. There were notes that only existed theoretically; like some particle scientist had tried to put an obscure theory to the test to find out how many black holes there were in the universe. After the fastest count-in he'd ever heard, sparks flew off the drummer's hi-hat and the bass guitar sounded like it would explode. Frantically, Arthur hit successive black and white notes as the bar lines zipped past his nose at the speed of light. The sweat literally dripped from the end of his nose. The trio didn't all finish at the same time. A glaring Spaniard pierced Arthur's soul. Clearly he was going to be the whipping boy. "Whatever else you do or-a don' do, we gotta finish all same time." Arthur feigned consulting with the other 2 in an attempt to buy time. He was assured that bass and drums had followed the dots exactly. Quietly, he asked, "Guys… just give me the nod when it's the last note." This they did and although it didn't placate the Salerosos, it got them through the night. Suddenly, the easy, boring gig at the George Hotel seemed the more attractive option.

Arthur stuck it out, though, and he found it got easier as the months went by. He was grateful for being able to work with Billy Fury, Marty Wilde, The Wurzels, Danny Williams, among many others, and his hero, Max Wall. Arthur had always loved Max's act and his sense of humour matched his exactly. He found it difficult to concentrate on the score while Max went through his zany 'Professor Wollofski' routine. Some nights the tears would stream down Arthur's face as he tried desperately to focus on the dots. He learned a great deal from this giant of a music hall legend. Timing, delivery, originality and comic genius were all wrapped up in this rather small and wiry frame. Arthur would use Max's influence in his own writing, art and music for a long, long time to come.

The 'phone rang. It was Leonard from the Merrye Men. Arthur knew he'd enjoyed a really successful career in music. Having formed his Art Movement band based in London, the whole group got the job of backing Roy Orbison, mainly through Leonard's contacts and an excellent group of musicians.

"I want you to be piano player for Roy," Leonard enthused. "We've got a European tour coming up and Roy wants a full orchestra. I'm his tour manager now… bass player too. Come to that, I seem to be musical director as well."

Arthur was speechless for more than a few moments.

"When's all this happening?" Thoughts of the Salerosos episode came to mind and he wondered whether he'd be up to backing the big 'O'.

"We rehearse all next week," was the enthusiastic reply.

"Oh, no. I can't do it Len. The job at the Toll House is a water tight contract. I can't just walk away from it."

"OK. I realise it's short notice. No problem. Hey - how about if you could drive Roy to gigs while he's in the UK? We could fit in your availability when you're not playing. I need someone I can trust."

"Yes. I'd love to." Arthur felt a sigh of relief sweep over him. No pressure. Meeting the great man… and getting to see the shows. Brill!

And so he collected and drove this super star to and from gigs. And Roy **was** a *'super'* star. He also had his father with him who was equally super and they all chatted about America, the wonderful reception Roy got throughout the world, Nashville, Leonard's sterling work and the Olympics. Then it was back to the Toll House.

The cabaret work, although very taxing, was very rewarding musically and financially. One Mike Ash, a would-be organist who had bought a Hammond organ from Arthur while working at Cranes, tracked him down and offered him solid, wall to wall work backing acts. It was too good to resist. Because all the gigs were reading music, the money was better than for busking jobs. Mike put Arthur with drummer, Tony Collinson. Tony was the greatest and clicked with Arthur immediately. He had that knack of reading music well but could feel music, moods, and understand quite complex cues instinctively. The Arthur Throovest Duo soon gained an awesome reputation round the clubs.

It was another golden age that would last 15 years. Arthur worked out that he'd backed some 2,000 acts over this period and he and Tony became the closest of friends. Mike Ash booked the whole spectrum of turns... The famous right down to the dire and dreadful. Mercifully, most acts were between passable to excellent and it was very hard work indeed.

It was normal by 1970 for clubs not to pay for a band call in the afternoon. So, the reality was that Arthur and Tony would be set up by 7.00pm on a Saturday and be expected to sort out all the music for five acts and be ready to start the show for 8.00pm. It was a nightmare. A typical night's entertainment might comprise a girl singer, a comedian, a magician, a speciality act such as a juggler or mind reader and a musical turn of some sort. Very often the sheet music was inadequate or non-existent and the cues would be thrown at the dynamic duo in the band room-cum broom cupboard at the speed of a dysfunctional Gatlin gun.

Thrown into the mix of this unfair work environment was the fact that the act or acts turned up late. It was quite common for the compére to announce a comic, a hand would then thrust a bunch of music onto Arthur's Hammond organ stool and a voice in the wings would shout a count-in... 1 – 2 – 1234. Instinctively Tony would pick up the pace and rhythm while Arthur used one hand to turn the first page and use the other to play the first notes that presented themselves.

These would be 4 hour gigs with a short break for bingo. The break was taken up with going through all the music for the second half. By 12.30am two pieces of soaking wet cabaret-backers would slump in the bar and sink 3 or 4 pints of lager whilst staring at the wall. It was unbelievably demanding but they loved it.

Some of the acts were spectacularly brilliant. They never got the recognition they deserved but were happy to make a very good living round the workingmens' clubs. Johnny Roberts would be one such turn. A ventriloquist. But no ordinary vent act. His dummy was a kind of punk teenager with a menacing face. He'd come on, rest the dummy on his knee and start telling good, clean gags which warmed the audience up. Meanwhile, the doll would be slowly sizing the clientele in a really sinister way. It was difficult to connect Johnny with the dummy; it was just as if the punk piece of wood had a life of its own. Silent. Menacing. For what seemed like an age.

Then suddenly – half way through one of Johnny's jokes – it would leer at a male member of the audience and start a stream of abuse aimed at this one poor chap. Arthur thought he must be a plant, but it wasn't so. If the guy had a moustache, the doll might 'say' "How long have you been sucking a rat?" Followed by "Was Hitler your father?" and so it would go on. Johnny would constantly try and remonstrate and chastise his prop, but to no avail. This 'argument' would then persist for some 30 minutes with the audience gripped by brilliant ventriloquism. The target male would eventually answer back and start an argument… but not with Johnny - with the dummy! It was bizarre and a bit scary. Johnny judged the timing impeccably. The man would invariably get out of his seat and come to the stage and vent his wrath at the doll -   not at Johnny! The climax came when the dummy created a pause in the argument to ask his quarry, "Do you realise for the past half hour you've been arguing with a lump of wood?" Tony and Arthur would play Johnny and inanimate punk off the stage quickly before the stooge could catch his breath. This was often followed by a standing ovation.

There were countless other acts Arthur and Tony backed. They're all now lost in the smoke-filled 'dressing rooms' of history and wouldn't be believed through written narrative alone. And there were no videos or YouTube back then to verify such anecdotal accounts. Who could possibly find credible Dennis Beards? A Tommy Cooper type of turn but with a deadpan delivery. He cut up mens' neck-ties as part of his magical bumblings. Marvello Blanco [Mervin White] broke watches and Ricky Last, the singing cobbler regularly ruined punters' shoes. He'd cajole a member of the audience to part with their shoes while he sang his cobbling song and pretended to mend the shoes. In reality, he put each shoe on his last and smashed it to smithereens with a lump hammer in time to the music. What astounded Arthur is that nobody complained or asked for compensation against any of these acts, even though a trail of devastation was left behind after their cabaret slots. There was no compensation culture back then.

The cabaret and club act work came to an end. It was the advent of Karaoke and TV shows which seemed to specialise in talentless drivel. Gone was the long, hard apprenticeship of theatre entertaining and the herald of the instant pop star was ushered in. The fabricated entertainment turned Arthur's stomach and he decided to have a go back in the glue machine business.

This was a mistake.

BACK IN THE STICKY STUFF

Whereas Arthur excelled in selling and designing adhesive applications, his experience and ability to actually put production machines into factories was somewhat lacking. The enterprise that presented itself was completely the wrong way round. An acceptable method of putting beads of non-setting gunge into the joins of giant air ducts had recently been established by the heating and ventilating industry. Perfecting the installations had not been established, though. Jethro Hollins had heard that the playing work had dried up and contacted him, thinking that this business would make Arthur a good living. It didn't even make him a bad living.

The notion was that Jethro would simply introduce an industrial manufacturer of mega-large ducting to Arthur, supply him all the machinery, valves, high pressure hose and so on. Arthur would then quote for the job and go and install it. It should have dawned on him really. He'd never been able to put up a shelf or change a spark plug, let alone fix a complex integrated adhesive installation into a major factory. One of the kinder directors of a company suffering Arthur's engineering shortcomings said, "It looks like you've fixed it with a coal hammer." An astute and accurate observation. Other production managers were not so kind. Their comments may not be committed to print in fear of litigation from parents of small children.

It wasn't entirely Arthur's fault. Although his work did indeed resemble a William Heath Robinson cartoon, the thick ooze supplied by the chemical formulators had not been fully trialled. It worked like this. A large, gasketted plunger was placed on the top of the thick sealant which was contained in a 25 litres drum. A pump, attached to the plunger then pumped the grey sealant along a high pressure hose to a dispensing valve. As the metal duct passed under the valve, a sensor would switch the valve on and lay down a bead of the putty-like sludge. It wasn't an adhesive. It was designed never to set so that as the ducting expanded and contracted, the compound would not rupture or fail. Good theory!

In reality, the substance was a very rudimentary mixture, consisting of nothing more than clay and linseed oil substitute. Had the manufacturers tried it out through a version of Arthur's device they would have gone back to their formula-written-on-a-fag-packet. A postage stamp would have done just as well for the formula, since it was 'Clay + Linseed Oil Substitute.' The constant downward pressure on the material caused the oil to leach out from the clay. When the fitters clocked on the following morning after the installation, all the oil was swimming about on top of the plunger, leaving a solid block of clay underneath. The whole shebang was rendered completely useless. Worse than that, it was beyond repair and beyond redemption. Nobody would admit liability. Arthur would be made bankrupt.

The first court case was at Warwick Assizes. Arthur couldn't keep the payments up on his Ford Sierra. Bristol Street Motors had decided to prosecute. It had become a criminal offence since Arthur had sold the car on but hadn't sufficient funds to pay off the loan. The cops came round to his maisonette, cautioned him, arrested him and took him to Solihull Police Station.

The two detectives charged with the charge of charging him were more like Laurel and Hardy than Holmes and Watson. They took hours and hours to write out a statement. Arthur could see that this might work in his favour. The syntax the Solihull sleuths used was not as Arthur had dictated it. It clearly irritated the illiterates, since they neither understood 'O' level vocabulary, much less how to spell any of it. Arthur flatly refused to sign it until it at least represented his verbal outline of how the car was no longer in his possession but he had no intention of not paying off the balance of the loan.

This was clearly an unknown gambit and could never have been in Mr. Plod's handbook of standard, acceptable statements. What made it even more taxing for our men in grey suits was the fact that a friend of Arthur's had heard of his plight and settled the account. Common sense should have told a person operating in common sense that the most sensible thing to do was to drop the case. That would be common sense, wouldn't it? The credit company had their dough now, nobody was owed anything and the new owner of the Sierra didn't have anything to concern him. End of chapter?

Nope.

Arthur milked the farrago for all it was worth. He insisted - as was his prerogative - to be tried by jury, much to the profound annoyance of Solihull Magistrates. The trial lasted 3 days and had it been filmed would have won an Oscar for the most outrageous fiction ever involving a court scene.

The prosecuting barrister strutted up and down like a peacock on heat, which itself provoked titters from the jury and he tried all he could to get Arthur to confess to some dastardly plot to deprive a reputable motor dealer from his cash. This also invoked some mirth from both the jury and the gallery. Bristol Street Motors must have been known to some of them. The judge had to order them to be silent on more than one occasion.

The barrister defending simply sat, smiling at anyone who caught his eye. After the pompous, protracted and excessively theatrical summing up by the prosecution, our quiet, confident defender of justice rose slowly to his feet, looked at the jury and stated, "If you think my client wilfully withheld monies or property from a motor dealer, you must bring a verdict of guilty as charged."

The judge looked quizzically at him. "Are you, therefore, suggesting that if the jury decides that there has been no desire on Mr. Throovest's part to deprive Messrs. Bristol Street Motors of either cash or merchandise then they should acquit him?"

"I am making that suggestion by implication, my Lord," was his succinct rejoinder.

Summing up by judges is always an intriguing affair. They always manage to 'direct' a jury in a manner that clearly defines how they, themselves, feel the verdict should be reached. In this case our no-nonsense arbiter of English criminal law left the court in no doubt about who the villains of the piece were. In as many words he told the police to consider the costs of bringing unwinnable cases to court, suggested that the motor trade might look to their own questionable practices and that prosecuting barristers might take counsel themselves before lumping law-abiding citizens in with the Kray twins, simply because they'd fallen on hard times.

After 3 minutes, Arthur was in the caff enjoying his favourite coffee with his very kind and relieved benefactor. The jury returned a verdict of not guilty and in doing so had opened up the next chapter in Arthur's life.

NICKED

Whether connected to the 'stolen' car incident or not, Arthur never discovered but very soon after this absurd piece of Solihull police work, there was a strange 'phone call. "Is that Mr. Throovest?" A rather refined voice asked.

"Yes," was the rather nervous and unrefined response.

"This is Bainsbridge-Wooley from the Home Office. I have been advised that you are a professional pianist. Would that be correct?"

"Er.. yes… I do play piano. Have played it… well, I still do play in a manner of speaking…"

"Then I would be most grateful if you would consider working for my department."

Arthur's mind raced. Was this a wind-up? Did the police want to get their own back? Doesn't the Home Office have cupboards full of piano players somewhere in Whitehall?

"In what capacity?" was the only question Arthur could think of blurting out.

"I need someone to head up a music department in HMP Fradley-Over-Edge. I have been advised that you would be ideally suited to the appointment. Could you come and see me this Friday at 7.30 pm?"

"Well… yes… I think so. Why me, though? I mean don't you have to have certain qualifications?"

"The profile I have here for you demonstrates that your qualifications are perfectly matched to the task in hand."

'Task in hand?' That phrase sounded a bit scary. Arthur hadn't taken up tasks in hand before and lurking in the back of his confused brain was a certain fact - as best as he could remember - Fradley-Over-Edge was a maximum security jail, wasn't it? All the headline cases seemed to be spending all their considerable time there.

"I could discuss the matter, I suppose," Arthur managed a slightly more cool reply and attempted to sound professional.

"Good. Then I'll see you at Fradley this Friday. 7.30 pm. The gatehouse will show you the way to the Education Wing."

"Fine. This Friday, then."

Arthur smiled to himself. What on earth was the Home Office thinking of? How did they know about him? Was he now on some secret file? Was he deemed to be one twelfth of the Dirty Dozen? Were they going to get him inside the nick and then somehow not let him out? It all seemed so bizarre.

"Throovest... I have an appointment to see a Mr. Bainsbridge-Wooley. He said you'd show me the way to the Education Wing."

"It's SIR Bainsbridge-Wooley, sir. An officer will escort you."

Seventeen half ton doors, walks underneath helicopter wire and twenty minutes later and Arthur was ushered into a room resembling the old masters' common room at Moseley. Bare. Utility. Unfriendly – as if every effort had been made to keep it as basic as it could be made. A smart-suited man rose from behind a desk, simultaneously placing a pipe on the plywood top, extending a hand and attempting an unpractised smile.

"Throovest?"

"Mr. - rather, Sir Bainsbridge-Wooley?"

"Well, it's either Sir Randolph or Bainsbridge-Wooley. Best call me Rudi in here."

Arthur couldn't quite absorb the logic or connection behind that but felt it best just to go with Rudi for the time being.

"It's quite simple Arthur - may I call you Arthur?"

"Yes... yes, that's fine."

Arthur felt like saying 'Call me Cedric in here' but didn't think humour was the card to play just at this moment.

"Government policy has swung back to insisting on delivering art and music into prisons and we want to get under way immediately. What I want you to do is to get those prisoners off the wings who've expressed an interest in taking music. How you take the sessions is up to you. If you can teach them something, then that will be a bonus."

Arthur felt a hint of ease and reassurance. 'Up to me' sounded unstructured. 'If you can teach…' sounded like no pressure. This was sounding plausible.

"How safe will it be?" Arthur found himself asking the question spontaneously.

"Oh, you'll be fine. There's panic buttons all over the place. Officers get to you in seconds."

'Seconds,' thought Arthur, 'Death only takes seconds!'

"So, can I ask you to start as soon as we've cleared you?"

"Well… Yes. Alright. I might as well."

"My department will send you all the details… Official Secrets forms, pay structure, hours and so on. The conditions will be excellent for you."

Sir Randolph rose, cupped his pipe in one hand whilst whisking his briefcase in the other, simultaneously rising, turning and exiting in one movement.

"I'll take you back across, sir," said a po-faced slash cap. And so he did. Another twenty minutes of clanking, jangling, squeaking and banging. Arthur was glad to be out and on the way home - via the Blue Boar pub and three pints of Hook Norton which barely touched the sides.

'Out of the glue and into the sticky nicky,' he thought as he pondered recent events; his life. Would anything in his existence ever start to make sense? He rather felt it wouldn't. But here was the prospect of earning some much needed dosh. The Home Office did look after its own, didn't it? It was music after all. Surely the guys would have something in common with him? Within a week he would find out.

A chilly Monday morning had our new Head of Music escorted once again across no-mans land to a security office adjacent to the main jail.

"Induction," said a dispassionate voice. "This will take all day."

Arthur wondered when he'd actually see an inmate, let alone impart musical knowledge to one. Oh well. The rather pleasant upside to all this was that he was getting paid for it. And paid rather well.

He sat through interminable briefings. Why he wouldn't be a key holder. What he couldn't bring in. What he couldn't take out. What he could tell prisoners, what he couldn't / shouldn't / mustn't. Each briefing had its own attendant paperwork. All had to be signed, dated, filed. Yet another Official Secrets Act agreement and then mugshots. 'If I'm treated like this,' thought Arthur, 'goodness knows what treatment the cons must get.'

They got it much worse.

The first day of actual 'teaching'. Fradley welcomed Arthur with open suspicion. The gatehouse officers must have practised for years at looking down their noses over a blank and expressionless face. Since most of them had come from the army, the technique had been learned early on; drilled into them. The Throovest flip-flops were the ultimate sign that this 'teacher' would be a constant target for expulsion. A threat to their regimen. Everything the regime knew about how to get rid of an incompatible would be unleashed on Sir Bainsbridge-Wooley's new recruit.

"You'll be in the Anglican chapel," said Shadwell Cadogan. "It joins with the Roman Catholic chapel." Shadwell was Head of Education. Ex-army and Welsh to the marrow of his being.

Arthur couldn't quite make out why there were two Christian-based chapels. He would learn that there were never two conflicting services, so one chapel would have done fine. "There's a piano in the Roman Catholic chapel, so you just have to wheel it through the connecting door when you want to use it," said Shadwell in a kind of dispassionate way.

"Is there someone using the Catholic chapel, then?" Arthur asked. There was no response - just a withering look which suggested he mind his own business when it came to the allocation of rooms and resources.

"Are there any instruments? Equipment?"

"You'll have to assess what you need and put a requisition in. Need to see what inmates you get and we'll take it from there."

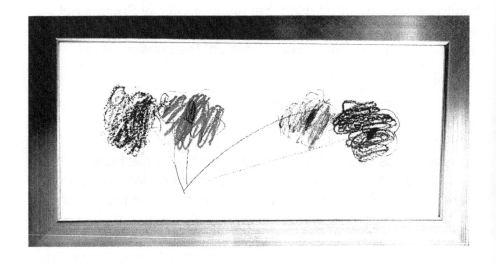

STIR…. CRAZY

Arthur, a piano and a quantity of prisoners! Suddenly our Head of Music was feeling a bit panicky. A dozen guys filed into the chapel. Some smiled and said 'hello'. Others made for the far corner and started rolling up smokes of dubious legal standing. Still yet, others wandered about as if enjoying a bit of space. An element of freedom.

"I'm Arthur," said Arthur. "Might as well find out why you're here." Stern looks pierced his eyes. "I mean - not WHY you're here. Why you're HERE… on the music programme." A big, smiling black guy sauntered up to him. "It's OK, Arthur. Relax. We're mostly just glad to be off the wings. Some of us play, though."

"OK. What is it you'd like to play?"

Suddenly the atmosphere changed from deep suspicion to deep interest.

"I was with a rock band."

"I did reggae."

"I write stuff."

Most wanted to do something.. did something. The tensions dissolved. A broader dialogue opened out into finding out what this whole thing was all about. The call from Rudi. The mystery surrounding the invitation to work in the nick. The fact that the Home Office now wanted an active music department. The discussions were animated, friendly and creative. Before Arthur knew it, the bell was ringing for the end of the session. "See you all tomorrow, then?"

"Yeah - you bet!" was the almost unanimous retort.

Arthur was swimming with ideas and good feelings. How on earth could such a (mainly) lovely bunch of blokes end up spending interminable years in a place like Fradley? Over time he would find out.

"Got it sorted, boyo?" Shadwell was testing Arthur from day two. A confident Throovest came right back.

"Yes. I'll need a P.A. system, three combo amps, a bass guitar, an electric guitar and a drum kit... for starters, anyway."

Mr. Cadogan's shocked face was a picture. "You decided all that after one mornin' did yeow."

"Well, yes. The guys want to get cracking. Might as well plug in to what they want to do. That way we can be sure they'll at least stand a chance of staying interested. I could bring my Hammond organ in. That would be great for the reggae boys."

Shadwell looked down at his desk. Shuffled papers. Hmm'd and haa'd. Muttered. Sipped tea from a cracked mug. Then suddenly he straightened up. "Yes. You're right. Sir Randolf wants music, isn't it? He shall have music. I'll get the chitty under whay this mornin'. Well done, Throovest."

The Welsh wizzard suddenly appeared to have had a moment of deep, volcanic revelation. Like he'd just won the lottery. Something had clicked in his ex-army brain that joined Home Office directive with what Arthur was about to embark upon. His eyes seemed to say, 'Prisoners off wings / box ticked. Music sessions starting / box ticked. Throovest seems capable / box ticked. Sir Rudi off my back / box ticked!'

The planning session was frenetic, constructively heated and argumentative. Throovest could see that the black domination was inevitably going to win the day. There were eleven black or brown faces to the three white ones. The white guys were cool about it all, though. The thought of having a live band and the possibility of doing live concerts, more than dismissed any notion of ducking out... even if it did mean playing reggae!

Days passed. Gear arrived. A routine got under way. The lesser able muzos graciously let the more able ones do most of the work. Arthur made sure that everyone got trained up, however, and even persuaded the star turns to teach the underlings some of the songs in their own time - of which they all had plenty.

The Regime was not happy about it all. Prisoners enjoying themselves and 'getting on' was not on the agenda. The uniforms themselves had very sad and humdrum lives by and large. The cons, on the other hand, were very colourful and, often, very talented. It was becoming clear that moves were afoot to get rid of Throovest and put the kybosh on what was becoming a very plausible noise emanating from the sometime protestant, sometime Catholic Rooms Of Hallowed Ground. Also, the number one governor had agreed to a Christmas concert whereby the Felt Collars would be the star turn. 'Felt Collars' was the brainchild of one of the less promising performers. His inspiration, readily adopted by the whole crew, gave him kudos and much-needed self-worth.

An uneasy atmosphere began to permeate the air. Nobody could put their finger on it, but attitudes changed and delays were orchestrated to get the guys off the wings and onto the Education block.

"It's too early for the Christmas gun," Wardrobe Jerry piped up.

"Christmas gun?" quizzed Arthur.

"Yes," added Al Seesaw. "They always get a grass to write a note and shove it under the Security Office door, saying that he knows there's a gun hidden on so and so wing. This gives them carte blanche to lock the gaol down. Hey presto… no Christmas concert. In fact, no Christmas anything!"

"Then there's the 'Carousel,'" chimed in Limp Wrist Percival. "The screws don't need any excuse to ghost blokes out to another prison. They knock 'em up and shift 'em at four in the morning. You just watch. The night before the concert half of us will have vanished."

Arthur's first reaction was complete disbelief. "You're winding me up," he said. "Surely they can't just…"

"Nothing we can do about it," shouted Lollipop Kreutz. "Just have to grin and bear it."

Arthur suggested an early mug of tea all round. "Let's take five," he said quietly. "There has to be some way round this."

"Tried everything," Charlie piped up. "Even threatened to burn the place down, but we all just spent six months down the block." The block was the solitary confinement wing and nobody enjoyed that experience.

The bell was about to usher the band back to their respective warrens. Arthur knew he'd have to come up with something to arrest the diminishing morale. "I've got it!" He suddenly gushed. "Could we make a guess at who might be ghosted out?"

"How do you mean?" quizzed Jerry.

"Well - if we had an idea who was going to be whisked away, we could cover them with somebody else. We've already got guys getting on swell. They're kind of understudies like you have in the theatre. If an actor goes sick, then an understudy steps in."

"I'm due for a spin," volunteered Seesaw. "And Kreutz is doing real good on bass… ain't yer?"

"I've never played in front of anyone, though," croaked Lollipop. "But I'd give it my best shot rather than cancel the show."

"That's settled, then," said Arthur, just as the bell went. "This is our project now. We'll have every instrument covered with a back up. I'll learn drum parts and bass, too, just in case."

"Yeah," said Lollipop. "It'd be about right timing for me to be ghosted. They done it before when they threw Al out of bed and into the wagon. Cover for both of us, Arthur."

The men all shuffled out with mixed feelings. Could they pull it off? Did they have the bottle to put on a show as the Felt Collars at very reduced strength and no advanced warning?

THE INCIDENT OF THE MARMITE

Life had a certain stability now for Arthur. He could play with the odd soul band, rock 'n' roll band and jazz trio while at the same time turning up for work at Fradley-Over-Edge. He was established at the prison and he assumed that the security guys were leaving him alone now. Presumably to turn their attentions on the band, rather than bar our very successful Music Head.

Nothing could be further from the truth.

Arthur had permission from Shadwell to take Marmite out of the gaol to give to a local church. The church sent it over to Romanian orphanages. It was no big deal. The cons got a jar of the black stuff every week and about 50% loved it and the other half hated it… just like the truthful Marmite ads. His initiative had the full blessing of the Number One, but the Governor hadn't informed security. After an afternoon thrash with the 'Collars' Arthur saw a carrier bag with six jars of Marmite in it, placed on his battered desk. This was unusual, because the guys normally gave him the stuff when they came up for lessons. No matter. Into his briefcase it went and off to be escorted through the interminable clanking of steel doors.

As soon as he got to the gatehouse, two of the nastiest uniforms jumped out in front of him and barked, "We're searching your case, Throovest."

On finding the Marmite, the slash cap with an oversized mouth connected to no brain shouted in Arthur's ear, "You're nicked." And reeled off a string of indictments, some of which forced Arthur to stifle laughter. Some of the accusations included stealing Her Majesty's comestibles, taking yeast extract from an unauthorised place [the kitchen] and not having a Gate Pass. The last item was, in fact, true. Even if you had a Government Issue pencil, you had to have a Gate Pass for it.

"Come in as normal tomorrow, Throovest," said Fradley's answer to Boris Karloff, after an hour and a half's grilling, "and we'll see you're sorted out."

As soon as Arthur arrived home, the 'phone was ringing. "What 'ave you bin doin' Arthur?" Quizzed Shadwell. I've 'ad the number one on the horn - from 'ome!!"

"I tried my best to explain to the uniforms about permissions to take the Marmite out, but they simply wouldn't listen," explained a shaken Throovest.

"I 'ad to laugh," continued a mellowing Mr. Cadogan. "Apparently, the slash caps took the jars back to the kitchen and chef asked if Mr. Throovest didn't want any more Marmite. The blood drained from their faces when they got the news that the number one was delighted you were doin' it for the orphanage. And 'ere they were in possession of the governor's gift. They've been hauled over the coals."

Arthur reached for the Scotch. Now the Fradley heavy mob were bound to find a way to get him hung, drawn and confined to quarters. And the concert loomed large.

CONCERT OR NO CONCERT?

Lollipop was the first to speak. "Al, Charlie, Limp Wrist and Wardrobe Jerry have all gone."

"OK," said Arthur, "Let's work out how we do this."

The guys looked worried and downcast. "Look, chaps. We've planned for this. We ain't gonna let the gaol rob us of the concert, are we?" Arthur felt like a football manager when the team was down 6-0 at half time.

"Arthur's right," chimed in Kreutz. "We owe it to all the cons - and some of the uniforms. Our wing P.O. actually apologised to me about it all this morning. A lot of others have been ghosted too. Seems like a job lot's been taken. The worst I've ever seen."

"Let's get down to it, then." Arthur was cooking. He got behind the kit, told all present what their instruments were going to be and as soon as they'd assembled he counted them in to their opening number, 'Knocking On Heaven's Door.'

It was a rocky start. "Don't stop. Keep it going. Don't worry about the finer points, just get the chords right. That's it. G, D, now A minor. Come on, sharpen it up."

After a couple of minutes the thing had settled into a gentle reggae rhythm. Some students from the cookery class poked their heads round the door together with Shadwell and a couple of friendly uniforms.

"That's great," shouted Mr. Cadogan. "I'll tell the Number One the concert's still on, then?" Arthur gave him the thumbs up, drumstick still in hand. All the guys in the corridor cheered. What was security going to make of all this? They were certain they were all going to get a night off with the cons all safely locked up on the wings.

Arthur made his way to the mess outside the nick. A po-faced, elderly cook just looked at him. "What's on the menu?" asked Arthur as cheerily as he could manage.

"Did you order?"

"Well… no," was the only truthful answer he could muster.

"Then it's cheese on toast."

Surely this woman had been the NAAFI's finest attribute in her day. Humourless. Blank. Cold. Unfriendly. A face that could disarm an enemy at 100 yards.

Arthur ate his unordered delicacy with the unease of a man about to go over the top. The quasi-military environment felt unnervingly apposite for the assignment he was about to undertake. Would they pull it off? Would he get the sack? Would security arrest him for eating un-ordered cheese on toast? His thoughts became more and more ridiculous as the fateful hour approached. And it was approaching fast.

The duty officer gave him a warm smile as he was escorted to the gym.

"The heating's still off, but all the Cadbury clan have arrived and they're having tea with the Number One, so they can't shut you down. The gaol would have to be set on fire to stop you now."

Although nameless to Arthur, this was a really good bloke. A kind of Barraclough character from 'Porridge'. There were some of his kind at Fradley.

Arthur stood alone in front of a vast, cold stage. The only person around was an old man who introduced himself as the 'man who'll be doing the P.A.' The gear was in disarray. It looked inadequate. The prison's musical equipment was strewn, nay, thrown all over the place as if somebody had strewn, nay, thrown it. Arthur's heart sank. The guys would only be allowed up when the visitors were sat in place. How would he make sense of all this and then be in a state of mind to put on a performance with less than an hour to go?

Just as he pondered the impossible task, the 'Barraclough' uniform appeared at the giant gymnasium door.

"Thought you might need help," he said with a broad, knowing smile.

"Well.. yes." Arthur was so taken aback, he didn't know what to say.

"I've got some men who will be watching over things tonight. They wanted to see the show so I suggested they come in early to do a 'security check.' "

He gave a wink and ushered in six, no, eight, big burly uniforms who made straight for the stage. "Where shall we start?" He looked like the side of the Matterhorn, but without the snow.

"It all needs putting together," said Arthur.

"Just show us where and how," was the most beautiful words Arthur had heard in his life. The officers lifted, shoved, swore, sweated and heaved like their lives depended on it. One younger PO sorted the P.A. system while the old guy just looked on with a vacant expression of no understanding.

"I'm in a band," the young officer proudly shouted across. "I'll get this lot sounding sweet as a nut."

"Yes, but which nut?" quizzed Arthur. The place will be full of 'em soon!"

Everyone laughed. The atmosphere became warm in spite of the room being bitterly cold.

"We've warned the Cadburys to dress warm," smiled Barraclough. "The number one's just told them the system's broke. It's not, of course." His expression simply implied what everyone knew to be the truth. Security had turned the radiator main valve off that fed the gym. They were the only ones with the key.

As the audience mixture of cons and VIPs filed in, the power to all the gear was ignited. Mikes? Working. Hammond? Working.

Combo amps? All working. The band ran up to the stage and stood, wide eyed at the professional set-up.

"Wow!" Exclaimed Kreutz. "It's like… for real, man!"

"These guys did all this," Arthur said quietly, motioning a discreet wave towards the officer roadies. "We wouldn't have been able to put all this together in time. They're stars and no mistake."

Lollipop ran over and grabbed each uniformed hand and shook it vigorously. Arthur was worried he was going to kiss one of them. This had never been done inside the nick. Although embarrassing, the team nodded graciously and hid behind the mixing desk.

"No chance of a sound check. We'll have to wing it."

"Nil problembo," was the cool response from Lollipop, looking like Clint Eastwood, about to take out 100 baddies with a Deringer and one bullet.

Wane Peterson - a strange, bright, intellectual con - opened the night with some poetry reading. This gave the band a chance to assess the effectiveness of the sound system and, more importantly, the mood of the audience. Applause was polite. Warm even.

Then they were on.

It was all a blur. Arthur was so focussed on pulling the guys together and encouraging them, that no sooner had the strains of 'Knockin' On Heaven's Door' kicked in, than it was all over.

It was like an hour and a half of concert had been compressed into a nano-second. There was thunderous applause. Friendly heckling. The wielding of huge, gymnasium benches by lifers who made them look like balsa wood. And then a tribute from the Number One and a gracious and heartfelt response by Dame Edith Cadbury.

Somehow liquor materialised at the back of the stage. Barraclough smiled at the lads and handed Lollipop a stack of plastic cups. Unheard of. The band needed no further invitation. It was a heady night and there was no other topic discussed for weeks… How the Felt Collars had given the gaol a show that would go down in history. The event percolated to all the other prisons and the absent friends who should have been part of the band that night at least had the satisfaction of knowing that they were all part of the victory.

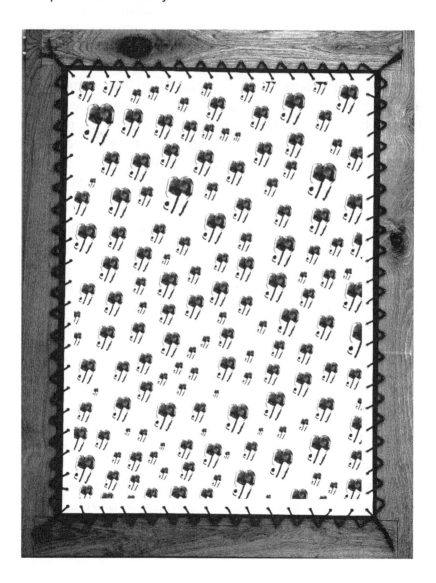

TAKING STOCK

It took a while for the implications of the concert to sink in. While he mused on where to go from here, he found that inspiration to write and record songs himself came from nowhere. The material was a bizarre and mixed bunch of stuff… the re-hash of old, traditional ditties and songs that just came to him. Without any kind of thought, he found himself recording numbers like 'Uncle Tom Cobbley' and 'Ilkley Moor Bah t' 'at.' He sang them in kind of laconic, Brummy dialect and wondered why on earth he was doing it. He wrote 'Happy Hatch' - based on the prison regime. It was an anthem to the treatment some cons got if they were deemed to be troublesome. Others followed. 'The Laughing Policeman' and 'Here's A Health Unto His Majesty.' Soon there was an album's worth and he pushed some cassettes out to friends with no other intention except that it would make them smile.

Shadwell 'phoned him up in the midst of all this and said that the Home Office had given him some time off with pay and had arranged for him to have a day at a seminar at the Midlands Art Centre. Although they didn't mention the success of the concert, it was clear that it was a way of saying thank you. The seminar was to be a meeting for those involved in education in prisons, together with folk who simply went into nicks on a voluntary basis.

Arthur arrived and was given his name sticker. It soon became clear that the couple who had put the day together had no idea about what went on in prisons. Neither had been inside one, let alone knew how the system worked. It looked like they'd put a proposal together to extract money from the government and when they were miraculously awarded the contract, they hastily cobbled together an itinerary for the day. It was a farce.

The culmination of this non-event had the group sitting in a large circle and being asked what they'd gained from the day. The odd bod chirped in with polite comments. Arthur just sat and smiled; at least he was being paid to be there. Diametrically opposite him there was someone else smiling the same smile. It was uncanny how so much could be communicated between two complete strangers at a distance, **sans paroles**. When the assembly dispersed, the two met at the coffee machine and introduced themselves. Arne Richards had been thinking exactly what Arthur had been thinking. It transpired that Arne went into prisons to take seminars which revolved around his Oxford Concert Party. The very title of the ensemble grabbed Arthur's attention. Arne asked about any work Arthur might be doing outside the nick. Arthur just mentioned the wacky cassette album he'd just finished. He wasn't really doing much else.

"I'd like a copy of that," Arne asked emphatically.

"I'll put one in the post." Arthur thought that it was kind of this gentle and obviously talented soul to want to hear his recordings. He also thought that he would never hear from Arne again. There was a cosmos of difference between a seriously professional harpsichordist and a Brummy rock 'n' roller, even if Arne did mix tango and baroque in the same soirée. He was convinced that the Throovest tape would be the end of the liaison.

Two days later the 'phone rang. It was Arne.

"This is the best thing I've heard for a long time," he gushed. "Send me six more tapes straight away. I've got a list of people who will love all this."

To Arthur's astonishment, Arne also wanted to pay for them. This was a first.

The friendship was bound to last. Arthur went to OCP concerts, joined Arne for some of his prison workshops and even performed at a Christmas concert at Holywell Music Rooms, Oxford, where the Oxford Concert Party trusted him with a zany spot before enthusiastic baroque and tango followers. His ample frame gave him the short straw to be Father Christmas too. The kids seemed to be suitably fooled. Arthur mixed a blend of

Vaudeville visuals with some of his songs and it was all very jolly. Christmassy. How seasonal celebrations can sometimes just work somehow.

FRADLEY PAROLE

Arthur's short sabbatical was soon over and it was on a cold and rainy morning that found him outside the gates of Fradley-over-Edge. The gates were normally open, but not this morning. There was a small side door with buzzer and intercom. Buzz.

"Yes."

"It's Throovest. The gates are locked."

"That's because the gaol's on lock down."

"Oh… I'd better go home then."

"No. You've got to attend security training."

"Nobody told me."

"That's because of security."

"What do I do, then?"

"Come to the gates. You'll have to be escorted over to Education."

"OK."

Eventually one of the huge gates swung open. "Are you Mr. Throovest?"

"Yes."

"I've got to take you over to Education."

The uniform seemed too young to be wearing a uniform. He looked like a school kid on work experience.

"Is everyone else from education here then," Arthur asked, partly out of polite conversation, but also out of curiosity. The place seemed unusually quiet - even for a lock down.

"Dunno. They just said to take you over."

After the ceremony of clanking, crunching, squeaking and

banging, Arthur found himself in the main education office. The lad locked him in. But there was nobody else there. Before Arthur had time to call back the uniformed youth, he realised that something wasn't quite right.

The 'phone. That was the only sensible option.

"Let's see... 'Security' - they must know what all this is about." Arthur mumbled to himself as the internal 'phone rang out.

"Security."

"This is Throovest. I'm in the Education office but there's nobody here."

"What the xxxx are you doing there?!" The voice exploded as if the very area was about to blow up.

"I was told to come here. You just escorted me over. What's going on?"

"You're in the wrong place, that's what's going on."

"Where should I be, then?"

"Hang on."

The hanging on seemed like an age. "Are you Mr. Throovest?"

"Yes."

"Then what are you doing there?" It was a different voice.

"You told me the gaol was on lock down but I still had to be here for some security thing."

"You're supposed to be in SP37... and you're late."

"How was I supposed to know? You brought me over here."

"This was an unauthorised escort. I never gave permission for you to be there. Stay there and I'll send someone over."

No sooner had Arthur put down the 'phone than a slash cap barged into the office.

"What are you doin' 'ere?!"

"I was brought over… but I think Security's sorted it now. I'm supposed to be in SP something or other."

Just then another figure appeared. It was the boy in uniform.

"Sorry Mr. Throovest. They said they told me but they never did."

"Don't come it," said the slash cap tersely. "Get Mr. Throovest to the right quarters. Savvy?"

"Where do I take him?" asked the timid escort detail.

"No good asking me. Ask Security."

The lad lifted the 'phone. "Oh, yes. Where shall I take Mr. Throovest? SP37? Where's that?"

There was another long silence. He replaced the receiver. "They're finding out where SP37 is, sir." The voice displayed anxiety, dented confidence and that kind of exasperation that portrays a sense that the boy wonder wished he was in different employment.

"I'll leave you to it." The slash cap disappeared with body language that said he didn't want to be embroiled in yet another Fradley cock-up. There were interminable cock-ups at Fradley.

The 'phone rang. Batman's sidekick nervously answered it. Apparently there was no SP37 in the book of known gaol rooms. He was ordered to take Arthur back to the Gatehouse while somebody tried to find out where the mysterious and fictitious gathering might be that should have had Arthur within its confines some 60 minutes ago.

"It's the new stores!"

The voice came from within the key room behind the gatehouse hatch.

"It won't be in your book yet. It was only finished 3 years ago."

A rotund uniform appeared with that ambience of 'I-don't-care-any-more-I'm-retiring-next-week.'

"It's there… look! The new building outside the window here."

The little knot of officers just stared at him as if they were just handed the most difficult and insoluble conundrum the world has ever posed. Eventually the most senior of them suggested that boy wonder escort Mr. Throovest to this new facility.

This he did to mumblings that suggested that governor grades might be emasculated, administration personnel were born out of wedlock and that those who teach music in prisons needed to abide in the cell with padded walls.

"Arthur Throovest," Arthur announced himself as he was ushered into the SP37 / stores / admin / Head Storeman office.

"We're a bit late, aren't we?" Suggested a smartly suited gentleman who sat behind the head storeman's desk.

"I was sent over to Education and then…."

"No matter," said the smart suit, "we're briefing the whole prison on security upgrades and we're re-training all Fradley personnel on Operation Clousseau."

'Clousseau' could hardly have been a better name. Peter Sellers' character matched the Fradley farce factory down to a tee.

"We can't recap here," chimed in an adjacent smart suit with Eton accent, "your department head will fill you in with the details. We've reached the delicate subject of substance identification."

There were a couple of civvies next to Arthur. The rest of the assembled company were all uniforms, two of them female.

"Now. What do you suppose this is?"

A dish of white granules was passed along.

"Could be salt, sir"? Suggested a smirky-faced officer.

"Or sugar," chimed in one of the women. The canny group of polished buttons chuckled under their disciplined breath.

"Well, it might be crack cocaine, mightn't it?"

The serious face of the non-Eton suit nullified the chuckles. "And how will we know the difference?"

"You can't actually tell, sir, that's always been the problem. If a con tells you it's sugar, you can't keep taking it away and asking a governor to get it analysed. You'd be classed as a fool."

The polite officer stated what all the others knew to be true.

"If you dipped your finger in it and tasted it, you'd know immediately whether it was sugar, salt or crack, wouldn't you?"

"Yes, but if it was crack, you'd effectively be taking it!" The female exclamation turned every head.

"We're not... suggesting... you actually.... dip your finger in a …. suspicious substance." Eton boy had realised the gaff and was trying desperately to find a way out. The group could, of course, sense it. They were onto it.

"So, how can we tell then, sir?"

Silence.

"We're just trying to point out vigilance. Yes. Vigilance is the key here. Be watchful. Vigilant. Keep your eyes open at all times."

"Or else we'll bump into something…. Sir."

The laughter was mocking but with a degree of restraint. These guys were from Clelend House. HQ. Big noises in the Home Office as well as the prison service.

"There's no time for levity. Look - if the substance looks suspicious, treat it as such."

Arthur thought he might as well make it known he was there. "I think we - all of us - would like to establish a modus operandi if we suspect we're looking at substances other than lawful ones."

Everyone just stared at him. "I mean there must be an official method of determining what the stuff is, without the risk of taking drugs?"

"Thank you Mr. Throovest." Non-Eton suit directed a firm and affirming look towards our flip-flopped Head of Music as much as to indicate someone was trying to make sense out of all this.

"Until an official directive is issued on the scenario in question, might I suggest that suspicious substances are left in place, a small quantity removed and sent via security to HQ for analysis."

"The thing is, sir," piped up one of the younger uniforms, "if we just leave the rest of the stuff in the cell and it's hooky, the con will soon get rid of it and there would be no proof to nick him on."

"Quarantine the residue, then," suggested Eton suit.

"But where? If we keep it in the office we'll be accused of supplying to cons."

"We'll have to discuss all this at a future date. We're already late for the next session. Firearms. You'll have the head of anti-terrorism to keep you up to speed with this one."

"This will be in the number two governor's office." A female in a very unfeminine black two-piece smiled at Arthur. "We'll find that easily enough. We all have to visit him goodness knows how many times every week."

The office had been cleared so that all the furniture was up at one end. Chairs were set out at the other and a wiry looking individual paced up and down as the trainees filed in.

"My name's X304 to you. I'm here to show you how a firearm can be made easily from materials you'll find right here… in the prison. Materials that prisoners can have access to." It seemed that X304 was trying to elicit gasps of awe from his audience. Everyone just stared at him. What was his point? You only had to work in the gaol for a few days to get to know that cons could make anything out of anything. Razor blades were carefully slipped behind light switches to get power to their radios. Batteries were expensive. Baked bean tins were converted into gin stills and melons could be made to produce a very fine rum. X304's introduction was stating the bloomin' obvious.

"This is a piece of gas pipe which anyone can get from the workshop. Place a smaller diameter copper pipe inside, block the end off and insert a small nail. Presto. A shot gun!"

Rather like an amateur magician, he then produced a cartridge, showed it to the group and placed it in the gas pipe. "Exactly the diameter of a twelve bore," he gleamed. Without hesitation, he snapped the two pipes together and there was an almighty explosion. The screams from the females would have been heard a mile away. One of them collapsed on the floor and one of the girls from admin immediately went to her aid.

"You xxxxxxx fool," she exclaimed. "You could have killed her."

"It's only a blank," offered our X304 like some kid who'd kicked a ball through a window.

Our supine lady in black groaned and was offered water from the number two's chilled dispenser. The tea trolley wheeled in as if on cue in some surreal Becket play. Perfect timing. Everyone grabbed a mug and stretched their legs, talking about anything and everything in nervous chatter.

Arthur now knew how to make a shotgun using materials easily obtained within the gaol's walls. But he was still unsure how to tell his crack from his saccharides… or sodium chloride.

He was beginning to think that this might be the weirdest day of his life. A thought that was to be proved exactly right.

One of the very workshops where you could nick two pieces of pipe was the next destination. The Cadburys were there already and it was clear that a demonstration was about to be engineered. This was how the prison sniffed out drugs. Literally. A beautiful spaniel was being fussed by everyone and a proud dog handler was chatting away to Dame Edith. A stack of cardboard boxes lay in a vast heap at one end of the workshop. The augmented group was at the other… the Cadburys and other VIPs made quite a crowd.

"OK officer." A loudish voice caused a hush to descend on the audience. It was a Senior Officer. "What's Nimbo going to do for us today, then?" was the lighthearted question.

"Locate drugs which are concealed among those boxes, sir."

"Did Nimbo see you conceal them?" A kind of conceited smile enveloped the SO's face as if the whole demo was a foregone conclusion.

"No sir. I hid the offending substance before I brought the dog in."

"Let's go then!"

Nimbo was let off its lead and within seconds reappeared from the cardboard mountain with a beanbag in its mouth.

"Well done, girl."

Applause and admiring comments gushed from the crowd. Dame Edith shook the dog handler's hand and patted Nimbo who responded with rapid wags of tail - like only spaniels can do.

The assembled company moved on and out to the next 'security' briefing. Arthur stood back and called the dog. Nimbo brought the beanbag over to him and dropped it at his feet.

"Quite a canine," said Arthur. "How long to train her to do that?"

"She's not actually that reliable with drugs," whispered the handler. With this lot here I had to make sure she'd find the stash, so I put an Oxo cube in the bag."

They both stood there and laughed.

"This whole thing's a farce," said Arthur.

"The whole nick's a farce," said dog man. "Be glad to get to the pub for the reality of a few pints."

"Get one in for me." Arthur slipped away and followed the ever-growing entourage.

Security's inner sanctum had never been open to civilians before. Even the Cadburys who, technically, had access to the whole nick had never set foot inside this chamber of horrors. There were medieval manacles, head restraints, truncheons, chains of various lengths and weights, all hanging from the walls as if in readiness to torture those of the liquid cosh. There was an eerie silence. The place was suitably dark and a slash cap broke the silence.

"This is mainly for the benefit of the officers here present," he articulated, as if addressing a wedding ceremony. "But it'll be useful for you all to know how we cuff and transport prisoners. Fradley always likes to keep the lads well trained. Could I have a civilian to act as a prisoner?"

Why everyone looked at Throovest, he'll never know. But they did and without his consent or even a nod of approval, the smartly pressed uniform beckoned our music man to the front.

"On long transfers we have to use this official method of restraint." A very long, jangling chain was lifted from its place of rest and strung out between two of the officers on the course. "Now. Show us how you secure a prisoner prior to transportation."

The two men just looked at him and clearly had no idea what to do next.

"I should explain that this will be a long journey… say to Durham or the Scrubs." He was giving the men time to pull themselves together and work out the complexities of the metal puzzle that had been presented to them.

"Er.. well… obviously we must secure the cuffs," offered one of our novices.

"Yes, but how do we do that with extended linkage?" Security man was beginning to look embarrassed. It was clear he should have rehearsed all this. The Cadburys were taking mental notes.

Then, as if a stage illusionist and magician had suddenly appeared, our master of secure transportation took Arthur's hand, swiftly cuffing it and manoeuvering it behind his back and bringing the other to meet it. Another manacle was then snapped onto one of the recruits and they stood there, umbilically joined, but four feet apart.

"On a long journey," interrupted Dame Edith, "There must be opportunity for either officer or prisoner to go to the lavatory. How do you deal with that?"

"Very simple, ma'am," was a more confident retort. "Without going into the subject in precise detail - not in mixed company, anyway," he attempted a laugh, feeling that he'd become a human. Witty, even. "Simply unlock your own cuff and lock it round the cubicle handle."

"And if there is no handle that will take the cuff?"

"Well, you just have to improvise… keep it on your wrist and feed it under the door. You just have to use your loaf."

"Loaf?" Enquired Edith.

"Yes, ma'am. Loaf. Loaf of bread… Head."

"Oh, I see."

Clearly she didn't.

Arthur didn't like to say, but the cuffs were very painful. He was just debating whether to raise the alarm when the assembled company was dismissed and a final session was promised. A session that was to be the icing on the cake. A spectacular even.

Everyone knew there was a command centre of some sort within the prison walls. Nobody ever knew where it was, however, and this was to be the final location and Arthur's group would have the rare privilege of witnessing it.

It was a bunker directly underneath the Number One's boardroom. It looked like it had been modelled on Churchill's wartime bunker in Whitehall. Indeed, it probably had been. Even the furniture looked like 1930s. The only things that belied anything remotely modern were four telephones. Not exactly state of the art telephones but not exactly pre-war either.

A suited, Home Office gentleman explained about the 'phones.

"The white one is a direct line to the gatehouse. Anything they think isn't quite right and they'll notify Command immediately. It's not actually connected yet. The black one is a direct line to the Number One's residence. He hasn't actually agreed that it should be connected... yet. The blue one, as you might have guessed, is a direct line to the local police station so that any law breaking in the gaol can be dealt with immediately."

"Oh boy. The red one." Arthur stifled a laugh as he thought to himself, "This is going to be a direct line to MI5!"

"And the red one," here it comes... "is a direct line to head of security at MI5. If a serious scenario presents itself which is outside of the prison's remit or resources, then our top security service will be drafted in immediately."

"Is that connected?" It was one of the admin workers who asked the question. Our suited civil servant wasn't sure if she was taking the mick. But his retort was stern and deadpan. "No. Not yet."

Then a rather large uniformed woman stood up, welcomed the Sirs, the Dames and a Lord, ignoring any kind of acknowledgement that riff-raff were present. She also paid no acknowledgement to the previous speaker. "This is Fradley's new Command Centre," she beamed. "It's going to revolutionise security within the gaol and this is where Clousseau comes in."

Everyone looked towards the large, steel, locked door expecting a Sellers look-a-like to come in.

"No, no. Not him," she burbled, realising her well-rehearsed speech would be useless from now on. "It's a software programme the Home Office have developed to sort out who's causing the trouble."

This statement was lost on Arthur. Everyone in the nick knew exactly who it was that caused the trouble. It was troublemakers who caused the trouble. The rest of the inmates either went along with the troublemakers or else gave them a wide berth. You didn't need a computer programme to work it out. And the brand of software was compatibility to perfection. The bumbling Clousseau would have been in his element among the bunglings of security.

The rotund officerette continued. "We're relying on you civilians. Report anything you see as suspicious. If a prisoner goes absent from your class, a church service or is seen talking to other inmates in dark corners. That sort of thing."

The flood of thoughts that went through Arthur's incredulous brain was manifest. Firstly, where had this woman been for all of her career? Everything cons did was suspicious. They hid £5 notes inside drinking straws. They were always going off during lessons, talked in dark corners, kept pot in the cookery room fridge, shopped one another, fought amongst themselves, fought with the uniforms and occasionally killed one another.

But the undercurrent of 'We're relying on you civilians…' was the straw that broke the head of music's back. A straw that might break camels' backs and camels were made of sterner stuff than Arthur. The position of being trusted by the men he served was now being officially undermined. He left the gaol that night, went to the Blue Boar and drank more pints of Hook Norton bitter than were good for him. He never went back to Fradley-Over-Edge.

Shadwell was genuinely sorry to see him go. He, too, was very unhappy about the new directive to actively grass up the guys who came onto education. It had been made plain that if no 'Clousseau' reports went in week by week, this would be looked upon in a negative light; not toeing the Prison Service line. It would soon be Mr. Cadogan's retirement, however. "I'll soon be out of 'ere myself." He had confided to Arthur with some disdain. "28 years and no time off for good be'aviour." It was an established gag among workers in prisons. Shadwell had always toed the line. Ran education by the book. Things had changed. Moved on.

HOME OFFICE AGAIN!

With the aspirations of fame, fortune and popularity all now a distant dream, Arthur wandered about aimlessly wondering what on earth he would do next. Instead of walking past Office Angels, he signed on with them and they gave him immediate work. The reason they yanked his arm off to start straight away was because he was Home Office cleared; had all the Official Secrets Acts already signed and in place. Across the road from them in Solihull was an Immigration Centre. They were snowed under with a backlog of unprocessed visa applications. They were even way behind in processing applications for employment there because this, too, required manpower they simply didn't have.

He arrived at 8.00 am and was whisked into an office by a tall Indian gentleman.

"Oh, thank you Mr. Troovist for your coming so swiftly, isn't it? We have so many foreigners wanting to come into our country and they are writing all the time to our Prime Minister and Queen about so long it's all taking. We'll show you how to process applications and would you please be starting now, thank you."

Arthur dismissed racist thoughts of 'foreigners coming into **our** country' and nodded his approval to get cracking.

His office was behind the counter where the public came to get their visas. There were several personnel working alongside him. A woman of grey dress and complexion was to train him on the two Home Office computers. The wall by the desk was stacked with passports and files that looked like it was part of a Dickens stage set.

"You take a file from the bottom of the pile," she instructed, "put the Case Number into the programme on this computer and ask for the Case History. If nothing comes up, go to the other computer and put in the applicant's full name and date of birth."

"I know this is probably a silly question so early on, but why can't the two operations be carried out on just one machine?" Arthur asked sensitively and politely.

"I don't know really. It's the Home Office, you see. They just do things this way."

" And taking files from the bottom? Could we not put those to be processed first on the top?"

"Now, that's a good idea!"

Arthur could see in part why there was such a backlog. Clearly common sense was not on the top of the pile either and there seemed to be no management structure. No clear chain of command. Since both computers were linked to a common, secure internet server and the programmes on the older of the machines could be loaded onto the newer one, he simply operated from the one machine. It was clear to everyone what he'd done and nobody said anything

The 'phones rang interminably. Nobody answered them. Nobody. He wondered who it was that was 'phoning so persistently. Whitehall? A minister? The Queen? He picked up a receiver at random.

"Thoovest, Immigration." He felt a wave of importance waft over him as he delivered his introduction in a pseudo official Home Office voice. It was a Chinese girl. At least she sounded like she was Chinese... and like she was a girl.

"I a student in Convently an' need extenshen to stay in Engrand."

Arthur realised he had absolutely no idea what he could - or should - do about it. He turned to his grey colleague. "Chinese girl probably. Extension of Student Visa?"

"Oh yes. Get name and passport and visa numbers and date. Head Office will send her an extension application. I'll show you how."

"Your name, prease. Sorry... please." Arthur was enjoying his resumed official voice.

"Ying Tong," came the repry. Arthur bit his tongue. The poor girl must surely have had a basin full of ribbing over the unfortunate association with Spike Milligan's famous song. "Is that spelled the same as…"

"Yes." The rejoinder came back swiftly. "Same as song tiytor."

Arthur took all the details as directed, found the programme to process them and made a note in a book he was keeping with all his training notes. That was easy enough. Van driver turned up, collected files duly processed, off to London to be delivered that night. The pile of files stashed against the wall having gone down a good eight inches or so. This was too easy. Surely?

"Where's this passport?"

It was 8.00 am. Mumbai Mike was both brown and puce. He thrust a piece of paper to our new recruit who duly looked at it with mystification.

"I've no idea," said Arthur. "Should I know?"

"You did all the processing yesterday, isn't it? This passport is to be collected in person this morning. Do you remember what you did with it?"

Arthur's brain just froze. He'd just followed grey woman's instructions. Isn't it? Then he focussed on the name scrawled alongside a passport number. He remembered it because it was unusual. The name was Prantil-Prantil Boutrros-Ghali, the same surname as a one-time Egyptian UN head. And the number was 0000007.

"Ah, yes." Our rookie suddenly gained confidence and composure. "This chap applied for full residency in the UK. In order to move his application along, it had to be ratified by Marsham Street according to the computer. He wouldn't have got clearance today."

Mumbai and the several faces that had now gathered round what was an obvious bit of excitement, looked blank. "But Mr. Boutros-

Ghali has come up from London to collect his passport, haven't they?" Our Asian office manager spoke in a monotone as if he was going to be taken outside and shot.

"Then he can go back to London," said Arthur confidently, "and go straight to Marsham Street, not passing go, not collecting £200 and he'll find his documents there. But it won't have been processed."

The blank faces continued to be blank. Had nobody performed this piece of administration before? Had he done it all wrong? One of the older clerks turned to Mumbai and looked at him quizzically.

"That's probably correct form, sir. That chap has a diplomatic passport as far as I recall. The Home Secretary would have to have a final say on any residency issues. We couldn't ratify that decision here."

Mike's Asian body slumped into a chair and he put his head in his hands. "I asked him to come here to collect the documents. It's my fault he's driven up from London, aren't I? What am I going to tell him. I shall be handed the sack, can't it?"

The awkward silence was broken by our elderly clerk. "We'll tell him that the Home Secretary wanted his papers immediately. They had to be taken at once to his office... by courier... at high speed. I know the aide at Marsham Street. I'll 'phone now and brief him on a plan of action."

"This is most kindness. I still have to face Mr. Boutrros-Ghali though."

"I'll see him." Eyes fixed on Arthur as if nobody had ever volunteered for anything before. They probably hadn't. "I'll tell him that I sent his docs down to London and I'd omitted to tell you - which is quite true."

"Thank you Mr. Troovist, sir, can't you? My career was to be tattered in shreds, shouldn't it?"

"No bother. Tell you what. Somebody bring two cups of coffee into the interview room and I'll make him feel important; which he is!"

"Brilliant. You're a good egg Arthur." Old clerk spoke for all of them and Arthur had a sense of being worth something. Well, he certainly was of worth to Mumbai Mike. It could have affected his future prospects. Who knows?

The days turned to weeks... and then months. Arthur hated the hot, stuffy atmosphere in a crowded office. He found himself standing by the only window the rest of the guys would allow to be open. He longed just to be free. To walk in fresh air. To be out of another institutionalised type of prison. He handed in his notice to Office Angels, Mumbai shook his hand vigorously and he was given the ubiquitous leaving card and a large bottle of brandy. Good stuff, too. He was sorry to be leaving some good folk. For all their humdrum tasks, they warmed to him and he to them.

BACK IN BUSINESS

A daily wander took him to Dorridge precinct. He had heard that there was a piano shop there and he just fancied seeing what the trade looked like these days. It was an age ago since he was an executive of importance at the Midland Organ and Piano Company.

He peered through the window of a small box of a retail unit. 'Surely it can't be!' Our newly released Home Office worker focussed on a tall, imposing figure who paced up and down behind a large desk, cigarette in one hand and a 'phone in the other. Yes, it was Ralantando Popodopolous. Arthur had recruited Ral as a salesman to work in the Birmingham City Centre store alongside himself and Ryland Skucheck. Ralentando was only eighteen at that time; he would be in his late fifties now and had hardly changed at all. The rather dashing Mr. Popodopolous spotted Arthur and with an expression of sheer delight, beckoned him in. They talked and talked about old times. Better times. Ral had married a young starlet… a whiz on the electronic organ and they were in business with a thriving teaching facility in a unit opposite.

"I want rid of this place. It's too much. I'm doing piano lessons and flogging joannas as well as running the whole teaching administration. Why don't you take it over. Just pay me for stock as you sell it."

"Why not?" was Arthur's immediate response. Another door opened just like all the other doors. Opportunism? Insanity? Opportunistic insanity?

Probably all three.

Arthur hadn't checked Ral's stock list to find out essential information. Like how much it had all cost, for instance. Since most of the rather run-down stock was second hand and put on the floor as 'Sale Or Return', it would have been useful to know who the owners were as well.

Arthur asked Ral over and over about who owned what and what it owed them. It was clear Ral had no idea. It was also clear that Arthur's one time junior salesman had dumped the shop on him to get out of massive troubles that were about to be unleashed on Arthur. The 'phone rang incessantly and angry piano owners flowed through his door to enquire what had happened to their beloved instruments. Whereas some were found to be still on the shop floor, others weren't. It was clear that Ral had sold stock, pocketed the dosh and not bothered to settle up with the source of supply. And there was no paperwork.

Our Throovest's Piano Emporium proprietor directed irate sale-or-returnists across the precinct to Ral's office in the teaching facility on a regular basis. Some would come back and pour their hearts out at how they'd been duped. Others tried to accuse Arthur as being a front for the crook and threatened litigation. He compensated a lot of them on the say-so of their stories - since there were no documents - and eventually he cleaned up the whole operation and re-stocked with class pianos.

Just below the veneer of Dorridge respectability lay a yob culture. Whether youths came in from outside of the area or not, Arthur never discovered. Larger knots of mostly male loudmouths conglomerated in the precinct just as shops were closing. It wasn't long before windows were put in, with broken glass and beer cans accompanying each other on a litter-strewn pavement. Dissonant alarm bells competed with police sirens. One Saturday night our despondent retailer went home, drank too much beer and picked up his e-mails. Mostly junk. Including one from SADDO CRUISES. Or was it junk?

STRAINS ON BOATS - AND GAMES

The mail asked if Mr. Throovest would like to take up an offer of a last minute deal to go on a river cruise down the Rhein. Arthur returned the message asking if Saddo's Silver Cruisers wanted a piano player. Early on Monday morning the 'phone rang.

"We just got an e-mail from you saying you're a pianist. Was it just a wind-up?"

"No. It's quite right. I do play piano."

"Professionally?"

"Professionally."

"You might be able to help me then," a slightly anxious Silver Cruisers' voice semi-croaked down a crackly line. "We'd forgotten that our entertainer on the Silver Danube has got 6 weeks' holiday. Starting tomorrow. Can you come out immediately to Brussels?"

"Yes, I guess so." Arthur was acutely aware that he was agreeing to yet another request to go along with someone's desperate plea for help without so much of a thought as to what was really involved.

E-mails and 'phone calls were frenetically exchanged and Arthur found himself standing on the platform at St. Pancras early the following day. Miss Silver Cruiser had told him to collect his tickets from St. 'Pancreas', which made him wonder how well versed this company was in all things travel.

A good friend had volunteered to wind down the stock at the shop and get the windows all barred up as soon as possible. Arthur felt this would be a good time to wind himself down too, and take stock, a tenuous parallel that made him smile to himself as he swished through the channel tunnel at high speed.

The Brussels' taxi drivers would all know where Heembeek Kade was, the Travel Liaison Officer assured him. Not one of them knew. A very old Mercedes driver with an equally old Mercedes thought he knew where it might be and they trundled off along the road following the river. After some 5 miles or so, the aged Walloon taxi man dropped our Ship's Entertainer off outside a yachting club, extracted vast sums of Euros from him and sped off in a cloud of thick, blue smoke. No ship. There was a long quayside though. The yachtists were no help. Much continental shrugging of shoulders and gesticulations but not much else.

Having been legally robbed of all his currency, Arthur decided to walk upstream and see if he could locate a 125 meters long vessel. He couldn't. After a couple of miles or so, a woman emerging from a health club asked if she could help in any way. He explained his plight and she immediately telephoned her husband. Her face lit up. "Heembeek Kade is back towards town. I'll give a lift to you." Arthur expressed profound gratitude and off they sped only to be dropped back at the yacht club. "This is it!"

"Yeah… This is it," Arthur said, half to her, half to himself. Then he suddenly remembered. He had the 'phone number of the ship programmed into his mobile. A dour Afrikaaner voice answered after ringing out for a minute or so.

"Silver Danube. You want something?" It sounded like a foreign version of a gatehouse officer back at Fradley.

"It's Throovest here. Replacement entertainer. Where are you?"

"Held up at locks. Be at Heembeek in about 4 hours."

'Four hours,' thought Arthur. 'It'll be midnight gone.' He sat on his suitcase as the sun set and he waited. And waited. Eventually the shape of a river cruiser came into view, turned round and moored. A gang plank was lowered and an elderly woman beckoned him to get on board. She was Gladys Cornwell, the Cruise Director, aided by Millie, a Maori woman and a jolly, bearded man who hailed from Southsea… Ronnie Wandsworth. "Ooh, you must be absolutely exhausted Mr. Throovest. Come and have some supper… and some wine… or a beer. I'll get your case taken to your cabin straight away then I'll show you where your cosy quarters are later. They're next to mine."

The glint in his eye gave our new recruit a distinct sense of unease. Ronnie was clearly one of those men who liked men. A lot.

No sooner was Arthur sat on a stool at the bar, cold lager in hand, than a client came over just as our Head Girl was about to engage Arthur in welcoming conversation.

"What do you call this?!" Was the loud and rude outburst from one of our highly valued Silver Cruise patrons.

"How do you mean?" Gladys gave him a professional, icy stare.

"We're supposed to be visiting Brussels, not seeing the incinerators and cement works of Europe."

He had a point. Heembeek was 100% industrial. A waste disposal centre on one side of the river and a cement processing plant on the other. A heated discussion followed whereby Gladys stonewalled the guy and let him blow himself out. "Get this all the time," Gladys muttered, just as if nothing had happened. Arthur's heart sank. Would there be 6 weeks of this, he pondered to himself.

There was a very unnerving similarity between Fradley-Over-Edge and the Silver Danube. It was a confined space. The crew were there mainly because they felt they had to be…
(for the cash). You couldn't come and go as you pleased.
The confinement produced continual frictions, arguments and disagreements and the cabins were exactly the same dimensions as a prison cell. Arthur thought it best just to keep out of the way as much as he could. This meant staying in his cabin if he wasn't working.

After overcoming his first night nerves, he discovered that the punters were actually a very easy going bunch. He knew all their requests, they bought him drinks and danced to his vast repertoire of pops from yesteryear, reliving their youth and early romances. Some joined in the deck games he was duty bound to organise. Saddo Inc. had provided a cheap and tatty putting set. It must have been all of 30 bob from Argos. In fact it was so pathetic that guests laughed and laughed, thinking that it must be a wind up. He managed to persuade the formidable Miss Cornwell to get the company to cough up 20 Euros to buy 20 jugglers' balls. He used these as boules in a deck version of the famous French 'petanque'. Actually, he felt obliged to come up with an alternative to the Crown Green Bowls that the ship gave him. The deck had a camber. The first bowl to be bowled simply careered off to one side, down the gutter and into the oggin. With the soft jugglers' balls, the missiles more or less stayed where they were thrown. The wrinklies loved it and many bought their own sets to take home.

A week soon passed and Gladys more or less let Arthur get on with the job. The only aggro he got was from the Dutch owners of the ship. They hated anyone being popular. And Arthur **was** popular. The ship company's CEO boarded one day and proceeded to be rude to everyone. There was an unpleasant exchange whereby our Throovest explained to Mr. Vos that his contract was with Saddo and not with Vos River Cruises. His itinerary was agreed solely with the Cruise Director. This didn't go down terribly well. Vos's idea for an ice cream party on the sun deck was for our entertainer to provide loud, disco-style music. Arthur assured our Dutch colonialist that such noise was not the expectation nor provenance of an older, conservative British holidaymaker. He had already agreed with Gladys that he would stroll across the deck playing continental melodies on the squeeze box. As hard nosed as the Silver Cruises CD was, she seemed to buckle under the demands of Herr Vos. Arthur went along with the disco option, made sure it was ear splittingly loud and achieved the result he sought… There were dozens of complaints.

Arthur seriously considered walking off at the next pontoon or lock gate. Saddo Silver Cruises blasted Gladys. Gladys blasted Vos. Some passengers blasted Arthur. The atmosphere was blue.

A meeting was called. Arthur just calmly asked whose cruise this was. Was it a Saddo cruise or a Vos cruise? An argument ensued which concluded nothing. The protocols were all at sea. Well, all at river, anyway. There could never be any kind of smooth passage. Although contracts were between Saddo and its personnel, the Saddo head honcho simply said, "Do whatever Vos tells you." Hence, if Gladys agreed an entertainment programme and Vos decided on something different, Arthur was expected to do what the arrogant Dutchman wanted. The climax to all this was when Arthur turned up in the lounge to do his nightly spot and… no sheet music, nor lyric sheets! No papers at all. No nothing. Having got a shoulder shrugging from all the bar staff, he went to our dour Afrikaaner Hotel Manager. "Any ideas where my music's gone? It's all missing."

"How should I know?" was the somewhat unhelpful reply.

"Well, you might have asked the cleaning staff to move it somewhere so they could do their job."

"That's housekeeping," was a further reply of equal unhelpfulness.

Arthur walked away, wondering what the plan of action might be. Just as he did so, a young Romanian waitress stopped him.

"I saw mister Vos with all music."

"How do you mean?" enquired Arthur.

"Saw he gather it in big armful," she gesticulated, simulating a struggle with two armfuls of heavy papers.

"Right. Thanks." This didn't sound good. Crazy Dutch person had now left the ship, so what on earth was he doing… had he done with our entertainer's tools of the trade. The scenario was conveyed to Gladys who very calmly asked the captain if his crew would try and locate the missing music. This he did. But just as the sailors were about to go on a search party, one of the cleaners piped up. "Arthur's music is in the broom cupboard, next to the galley. I saw Mr. Vos throw it in there."

There were mystified looks. A few crew members, together with Arthur, followed her down the stairs and - voila! - a heap of papers strewn all over the broom cupboard floor.

"Will you sort this, Gladys, or shall I?" Arthur's question was brief, cold and determined. "Don't worry, Arthur. I'll deal with this."

The show started late. The punters soon got into the swing of the evening's entertainment and Arthur did a quiz to supplement the lack of an organised programme.

"Apparently, Vos threw a strop over your stage area being untidy." Gladys peered at Arthur over her early morning coffee cup. "Just picked up all your music in a rage and stormed off."

"How did he think I was going to work properly without all that?" A good question.

"Just wanted to give you a hard time. Hates folk who stand up for themselves. Popularity, too. He hates that. Anyway, I've got some bad news, I'm afraid Arthur."

Arthur was expecting the sack anyway. He didn't fit in with the 'yes' profile of subservient Saddo / Vos workers. Suddenly, life back in Blighty felt like a lovely dream.

"There's a jazz week on starting tomorrow. You won't be needed. Saddo's efficient administration machine had forgotten all about it. They've asked if you wouldn't mind staying on the ship. It'll be cheaper than sending you home for a week and then bringing you back. You'll be paid as normal."

"That's fine," said Arthur. "Maybe I can sit in with them occasionally?"

He was laughing like a drain on the inside. How could anyone get something so wrong. It would be wonderful to have some time to himself. And paid for it.

The band was a delight. A Jools Holland tribute band of seven members headed up by a Miles Treadwater. They were all there just for the fun of it and Arthur enjoyed non-stop merriment as they played, sang, drank, mooched and laughed their way through a week of jazz and boogie woogie. Miles was a super boogie player and the others just read their parts in varying degrees of ability and competency. It transpired that Miles put a bid in for the jazz week slot, got the job and then had to put a band together in order to fulfil it. Our forgiving audience loved it and forewent walking sticks and zimmer frames to Charleston and Black Bottom on the postage stamp-sized dance floor every night. Arthur guested for some of the time and the band really enjoyed his style of energetic syncopation. The time flew by.

And soon the six weeks of our cruise entertainer's tour of duty was drawing to a close. It had been a mixed bag of fortunes. Great times. Hard and difficult times. The scenery and weather had been fabulous. The regime, not so fab. The point of departure was Cologne. A trip down a Merrye Men memory lane was inevitable. The Storyville Club was long gone; the district derelict. Arthur took snaps of himself in places and in simulated poses from all those years ago. He still had all the photographs from those heady days. Same buildings which hadn't aged at all as a backcloth against a muzo who **had** aged... and he was feeling his age too.

The trip home involved cramped and crammed mini-bus, followed by a packed coach and then the Eurostar back to St. 'Pancreas'. What would he do next? Nothing was in the diary, nothing on the horizon, nothing firing ambition, optimism seemingly Tippexed out of his very soul. Soon he was back in Blighty and he slept for two solid days.

The Summer dragged along somewhat. Some gigs came in… mainly for playing in care homes. He found these not to be the dreary jobs they at first sounded. Although the serious Alzheimers' institutions were hard going, the 'senior living' accommodations were rather rewarding. They weren't called Old Folks' Homes anymore. The PC brigade tried heavy disguises to make it easier for relatives to put their ageing relatives away. So Arthur was working in Rose Garden Eventide Villas, St Andrew's Mews For The Not-So-Young and Dr. Fernbaum's Silver Retreat. Why not 'Look, You're Past It, Incarcerations' he thought, and laughed out loud as he trundled his gear into another Darby & Joan Mansion.

But it was rewarding, if only for the occasional 'miracle' that resulted from his lively sing-a-longs. During a boisterous rendition of 'It's A Long Way To Tipperary', one old girl struggled out of her wheelchair and proceeded to dance a kind of jig. Two nurses immediately ran across to her aid and realised she didn't need any help. They came over to Arthur after the session and were quite moved.

"Alice has never once got out of that chair unaided since she came here… six years ago."

The Throovest magic often worked like that. Many of these dear old souls would be genuinely very grateful for his shows. They sang songs they hadn't sung for sixty years and more. They laughed and heckled and took very long trips down even longer memory lanes. Arthur loved it. Soon it was Christmas and there was a mail from Saddo Cruises.

A SEASON IN THE SUN?

They had expanded their river fleet. The regular guy on the Silver Danube was going onto the new ship - The Golden Danube - and did Arthur want to do a season on Vos's ageing tub? With no other prospect in sight, he felt he had no option. He persuaded Saddo HQ to write a clause into his contract stating that all directives concerning his duties must come from England and not Holland.

So, he closed his diary for the year, packed a huge trunk and awaited the Saddo van to come and collect all his gear. He flew out this time. Amsterdam was the start of the season but the Saddo team joined the Silver Danube at Arnheim where it had received a lick of paint and not much else.

The new sailing crew had already unloaded all the gear and it was a strange feeling setting up all his gear in the ship's lounge - PA system, two keyboards and various amplifiers and racks - and the knowledge that it would stay in place for the next eight months. The Saddo contingent was headed up by a Dutch guy. He couldn't have been more different from ship owner Vos, however. Jakob was congenial, thoughtful, multi-multi lingual and helpful. Arthur outlined his itinerary for the whole season and Mijnheer Jakob Sneek simply said "That's fine." Surely this was going to be a good gig.

Jakob's little helpers were two older women from the UK who had been friends with each other for donkeys' years. Both had been in the travel industry for ever and they knew just about everything there was to know about 'working your passage.' They talked interminably about places in the world they'd worked, clothes, currency exchange rates, men they'd avoided, men who'd avoided them, how Saddo should change their ways and incessant advice to poor, long suffering Jakob.

Jakob gave them the tasks of marshalling the guests around, which they did with the grace and arrogance of a primary school teacher at playtime, while he hid in the wheelhouse and gave excellent commentaries as the old vessel plied its way up the Rhine. On the first morning, the plying became more of a grunt and tussle, however, as sand barges and scrap metal tugs were now overtaking our '3 star cruiser with 4 star service.' A Romanian sailor dashed from the Danube's blunt end, shouting incoherently in the direction of the bridge. The captain ushered him in to his domain of supreme command and Jakob exited hastily to join Arthur on the sun deck.

"Problem?" asked Arthur.

"Big trouble, I suspect," answered a worried looking cruise director.

"The starboard gear box isn't working. Captain Sensible didn't even notice that the rev counter was going wild, but there was no thrust. He's been on the sauce and I don't think he's capable of sailing this thing. I had to point out that we're doing 3 kilometres per hour instead of 11. He used some Dutch I haven't heard for a while and now the engineer is going to have to try and convince him we've got a massive problem."

Arthur's heart sank. First day and the season looked like lasting for 24 hours.

"What on earth can we do?"

"Well. The first thing is that I'm obliged to tell Saddo HQ immediately that 'Houston, we've got a problem'."

The Black Pig limped upstream to the first pontoon available. The customers were confused and realised something was wrong but they didn't quite know what. And since the sozzled commander hadn't ventured to make any announcement, Jakob plucked up courage to get on the PA and try and make light of what was a cruise-stopping incident. He explained that there was a technical problem and he'd keep them informed as to progress. He tried to lighten things up by announcing free champagne at the welcome dinner that night.

Arthur was now well versed in all things ship-lore and he played his usual set of pre-dinner, guest-welcoming music. He had developed a knack of starting off with cool bossa novas, gradually cranking the music up to something perceived as 'exciting.' In this way, he could invariably bank on getting good applause just before the call for dinner. Something like 'Chatanooga Choo Choo' or 'The Good, The Bad & The Ugly' would be excellent choices to finish with. This served him well. The punters felt they were getting to know him, they gained confidence in his ability to play competently and this first 'performance' was a good 'ice breaker' with some easy chat and corny gags thrown in. The smiles on the Team's faces were a bit strained, however. The evening would be OK, but what on earth will happen tomorrow. They all went down to the restaurant, awaited the soup and hoped that HQ had come back to Jakob with ein meister plan.

GEAR BOX OF DOOM

Before daylight, there were the sounds of clanking, bashing, crashing and crunching. Arthur peered through the rusty-framed porthole to see a blue transit van being unloaded by dark figures. Realising there would be no more sleep, he decided to go take a look. Jakob was already on the quayside, furrowed brow and head scratching already well in place. The team of marine engineers had already taken the gearbox apart and were loading pieces of broken bronze, steel and cast iron into the van.

"It'll be at least three days before they can fix it," muttered Jakob. The vision of three long days and what to do with 120 newly boarded cruisers was imprinted into his sunken eyes. Arthur had one of his inspirational moments just like he enjoyed back at the Immigration Centre.

"Let's bus them everywhere!" It just seemed to spring from his lips. Jakob looked at him for what seemed minutes, a blank, formless face denying he had heard anyone speak. Then suddenly a smile cracked the morbid, Dutch face just as the dawn and twilight welcomed the day. A bird tweet-tweeted and the blue maritime ambulance sped away.

"Yes… busses. That's how we'll do it."

Jakob looked like a new man. Over bacon and egg, he rolled out his action plan to the bewildered Saddo girls. Arthur was already ahead of him. "Three coaches today will get them all to Rudesheim. Arthur, would you go with one, and you two take the others. I'll stay here and work on the itinerary for tomorrow."

The girls looked shocked. Something had happened that shouldn't happen. It was as if Jakob was asking them to take a shuttle to the moon - and not necessarily to come back.

Can it only be women who would say things like,

"This isn't on the schedule."

"What will the passengers think?"

"Can't we get another boat?"

Jakob simply smiled, made his way through the crowd of breakfasting guests and picked up the microphone. He was exuding confidence and it came across splendidly.

"You will have noticed we've not left the mooring," he gushed with a chuckle. "This can only mean one thing. The technical problem has not been resolved and the bad news is that the wonderful Silver Danube is staying here for a few days."

Groans.

"But I have some very good news. We're taking you to Rudesheim by coach today - much quicker than if we'd sailed there. And I shall be taking you to additional places that we couldn't visit at all if we stuck to the schedule. Free wine tasting. A five star restaurant in the Black Forest and an additional cruise on one of the many lakes around here. As long as the paddle steamer doesn't break down!" Jakob laughed. Nobody else did. But the gentle hum wasn't hostile. The punters were going to go along with it.

"Thanks Arthur." His steely gaze towards our entertainer was as if he'd been given a winning lottery ticket. Or maybe an Olympic Gold Medal.

"No trouble," said Arthur, "but I didn't see you organise any of this yet."

"I haven't. But HQ has given me a carte blanche to do anything at any expense to salvage the cruise. We can have some fun into the bargain." The girls seemed to warm to the idea of 'having some fun' and soon the coaches arrived to whisk them off to Rudesheim.

WHAT SHALL WE DO WITH THE DRUNKEN SAILOR?

It was a mystery to everyone how Captain Sensible was still at the helm. It was obvious that this young, ex-navy chap was pickled most of the time. His arrogance matched that of the ship's owner and, inevitably, his judgements were impaired, to put it mildly. It transpired he was a friend of the Vos family and there was no danger of him being shown the plank. He was a kind of mole… on the 'phone incessantly to Vos, telling him just about every detail about everyone and everything. Jakob picked all these conversations up, of course, and was disgusted that our dashing, young inebriate criticised and put down everyone except himself. The fact that Vos was just as bad made for a very unhealthy atmosphere on this ageing and ailing vessel.

The days zipped by. The gearbox got fixed. Loud cheers. Jakob declared a hero by the guests and Arthur played his heart out. The true British spirit had melded with a true Dutch spirit and a battle had been won. Even in torrential rain, Arthur insisted the ice cream party went ahead on the storm deck. Zimmer frames clattered under a great PVC canopy, Arthur got the squeeze box out and First World War songs were sung so loudly that they could be clearly heard in the neighbouring German villages. Dutch spirit was still being consumed by our helmsman in greater quantities, however, and the Saddo team were getting more than a little concerned about Sensible's ability to steer the ship.

The ship soon reached the Danube with no further mechanical failures. Our legless commander had never navigated the Danube before, so Vos had hired two 'highly experienced pilots' to take the vessel to the Black Sea. The two sailors turned out to be a couple of Romanian fishermen who couldn't speak any language other than Romanian. This was a big problem. Captain took the opportunity to let them get on with sailing these uncharted waters while he sank a few more in his cabin.

"BRIDGE"....

"Over" ...

"TROUBLED WATERS"

Arthur was enjoying one of his deck games of 'Boules' with a merry bunch of guests. Being windy, the 'pitch' he chose was behind the wheelhouse. All he could hear from inside this domain of command was one of the Romanian pilots. He simply repeated, "No speak English. No Speak Deutsch."

It didn't take a genius to work out that the river authorities were checking on the ship's progress. Security of navigation on all European rivers was tighter than even airport security. Every metre of navigation had to be accounted for and all manoeuvres involving other craft had to be meticulously planned, agreed upon and executed. It was clear that our foreign pilot was busking it. How long would it be before a police launch flagged the tub down? The icing on the cake would be if the licenceless and legless captain was in the wheelhouse with the licensed and incoherent Romanian when the Wehrmacht stormed the ship. These thoughts flashed across Arthur's slightly worried brain.

There was no challenge. No flashing blue lights and as the Silver Danube slid down towards the Black Sea, evening came, dinner was eaten, Arthur played a set of rock 'n' roll and the travellers were merry, happy and - well - merry.

The itinerary was tight, which meant that the ship had to travel through the night most nights. Hence, two pilots were essential. Captain would be in the wheelhouse with one of the Romanians through the night. He'd sleep it off during the day.

Ssssshhhhhh, bang! Arthur was thrown out of his bunk onto the floor, all the quiz papers, golf equipment and a shelf full of toiletries landed on top of him. The Black Pig was motionless. His watch said 3 am. There was no alarm signal, but our slowly waking entertainer knew that didn't mean a thing. He heard one of the Saddo women shout to her friend, "It's only a sand bank."

This explanation seemed good to Arthur. He heard the engines rev up again and he peered through the porthole to see the ship reverse a few hundred feet and then power up forward again. Sleep was uneasy. Breakfast time had the sand bank stories in full spate, but it was all light hearted and jovial. Jakob told folk, quite truthfully, that grounding on the Danube was a regular occurrence and the central channel of the river was, indeed, only sand.

The banks of the river were, however, rocks. Big, jagged rocks. Rocks that went down well into the river.

It was several days before it happened. 3 am again. Very loud crunching and a sudden stop. Arthur had rearranged everything so that it was now all on the floor. So when he was thrown out of bed, he landed on top of the golf gear rather than the golf gear falling on him. It was just as painful, though. Should he get up? He felt that he just couldn't be bothered. Whatever miscreant behaviour the sailors had been guilty of would be expounded over bacon and eggs in the morning. For no apparent reason, Stanley Holloway's 'Albert And The Lion' came into his thinking… "There was no wrecks and nobody drownded, if fact nothing to laff at at all."

He chuckled. Sleep soon overtook him.

The morning's conversations were a little more subdued. Apparently, one of the passengers had been in the bridge - another looking out of his port side cabin window. The guy in the wheelhouse had gone for a night time smoke. It was the only place out of the elements where anyone was allowed to light up… all three sailors were heavy smokers. The chap in the cabin couldn't sleep and was simply admiring the moonlit scenery. Our command centre witness explained that Sensible was at the helm at the time of the crash. One of the pilots had shouted at him, "Verlangsamen!! Verlangsamen!!" Excellent German this time, which captain spoke fluently and would have understood 'slow down' perfectly well. But the Dutch arrogance kicked in and he completely ignored the directive. Our fag-smoking passenger then outlined the sequence of events.

There was an island dead ahead. Captain referred to his charts while Romanian made it clear that navigable passage was by taking the left hand channel. Captain, of course, didn't take any notice and would make that decision himself. When 40 tonnes of steel, travelling at 17 knots, downstream needs to be turned, it has to be done with considerable forward thinking. 2 seconds isn't enough to avoid an island and changing the ship's orientation by some 90 degrees. The craft ploughed through the pointy end of the island, ripping out trees and branches as it did so. Our cabin witness saw a silver birch swing by his window, then he noticed the rocks. They got closer and closer until they were so close that he dived back into bed and awaited the inevitable.

How was Pugwash going to brush this one off?

Absolutely nothing was said. No announcement. Nothing. Jakob was pondering what role he should take in all this. A truthful PA announcement would undermine the protocols of command. He was obliged to tell head office. And he told our unusually sober captain that this was unavoidable. Sensible reluctantly agreed. But he said that he didn't want Vos to know. "That's up to you," said Jakob and left it at that.

The night soon came round again and it was party time. Not for the guests, for captain and his maritime crew. It was a night when the ship would be moored in Szigetszentmiklos. So, a night off from sailing was the order of the night and as Arthur played his way through his vast repertoire, all heads turned to see the sailors, headed up by Capt. Jack Sparrow march down the gang plank, boxes of beers, vodka, food stuffs of every kind and a giant barbeque rig. It didn't exactly instil confidence into the guests. They were all in civvies, in high spirits and in toxicated. And who's in charge when they're not on board?

Clearly Jakob was not happy. The travellers and our Saddo girls were all restless.

10.15 pm. All power failed. The music stopped, dancing stopped. Everything stopped. Emergency lighting came on and everyone just sat and waited. It only took a few minutes before what looked like a Captain Hook Tribute Group stumbled up the gangplank and vanished into the bowels of the Jolly Roger. Still no power.

It was a long night. No showers, no toilet flushing and no ventilation. Most of the cabins didn't have opening windows, so the air was like that of a stranded submarine. The morning couldn't come too soon. Jakob had quietly gone on the offensive ahead of the game. Coaches arrived pronto and soon the whole of the ship's company and caboodle were whisked off to Budapest.

The rock crunching from the previous day had put a hole the size of a football in the front of the hull about 2 feet below the water line. Captain, of course, hadn't bothered to check the engine room and infrastructure. Consequently, water had ingressed into the ship, eventually finding its way into the fuel supply and generators. Wait till Vos heard about this.

There was a miraculous ability that Saddo Inc. possessed. No matter where the ship was located, they always had a local agent who could sort out the most complex of problems. How do you get 135 holidaymakers booked into the same hotel at one hour's notice in the holiday season? Well, 135 people did all get booked in. To a five star mansion of a place. And it was just as if they'd been expected all week. The guests were all somewhat relieved. The hotel served the most wonderful food, had terrific amenities and… their own entertainment.

"It'll take days to repair the hole," muttered Jakob to Arthur over a cold, Hungarian beer. "Tell you what. Fly back home for a few days. I'll clear it with Saddo. They'll be so preoccupied with all this they won't notice the odd plane ticket. The hotel has given us their cimbalom player for as long as we need him. The punters will love a bit of local culture."

"You sure?"

Arthur thought they might tell him not to bother coming back.

"It'll be fine."

Arthur booked online and got a cheapo seat with Ryanair. It was to Luton, but no matter. There was a coach service to Birmingham. Soon he was drinking coffee, looking out at the pouring rain over Brum and wondering if he actually would get the summons back to the ship.

HELLO VIENNA

The summons soon came. Vos had to bribe ship workers in an ageing, Eastern Bloc shipyard to fix the ailing craft. Since it involved lifting the old tub out of the water, it was excruciatingly expensive. After five days, the Silver Danube was well on the way back to Vienna with all crew, staff and customers present and correct. Saddo e-mailed Arthur his flight details and didn't even bother to query his absence. Jakob clearly had done a subtle job in giving a much needed break to our bemused entertainer.

The cruise continued just as if nothing had happened and Arthur lurched into his full repertoire of musical soirées, quizzes, deck games and accordion selections.

As the patched-up Silver Danube weaved its way back towards the North Sea, Jakob delved through the interminable Saddo paperwork, updating just about everything that was updateable. He glanced across the lunch table-cum-office and gave Arthur a quizzical look.

"Did HQ tell you about the jazz week?"

Arthur smiled. "The last time a jazz week was mentioned, I was told I wasn't needed. Stayed on the boat, though."

"Well, it starts next tour and it says here you're to fly back home. Did they mention anything"?

Of course, nobody ever mentioned anything of significance. Air tickets were hastily arranged and soon Arthur was off yet again back to Blighty, taking advantage of spending a day in Frankfurt. The plane touched down at Birmingham International, he switched on his mobile and a text was awaiting him from Jakob.

"How thoughtful," he thought. "Jakob wishing me a swell break."

'Ship caught fire. 3.00 am. Everyone evacuated from the middle of the river and the middle of nowhere. See the News.'

At first, Arthur smiled. Dutch humour wasn't brilliant, but this was a good attempt. As he walked through the arrivals he looked up at the information screen near the car hire desks.

'Rhine river cruiser ablaze. No fatalities but several passengers retained in Dusseldorf hospital.'

He felt the blood drain from his face. He 'phoned Jakob's mobile immediately and was given a blow by blow account of a total disaster, except maybe that there were no deaths. Captain Sensible had been at the helm. The Night Watch was vacuuming instead of watching and the galley was on fire. Fire alarms didn't work and when someone eventually discovered the conflagration, our professional, level-headed commander refused to sound the alarm. Apparently, he muttered, "If I do that, it'll wake everyone up."

It was a statement that made its way into the police report. It rather dented the Vos empire's somewhat already heavily mutilated reputation, a reputation which had never instilled confidence in the maritme authorities.

Mercifully, the worst casualties were mild smoke inhalation and Saddo moved swiftly and big time to sort the mess out. An operation that was highly commended by just about everyone.

The upshot, though, was that Arthur would not be returning to be ship's entertainer.

FORTUNE?

He sat in his modest abode, sipping a rather inferior English lager, pondering over his strange life. If he'd been a bit less obliging, might he have enjoyed a taste of fame? A modicum of fortune? A tiny piece of prosperity?

The disjointed episodes wafted over him like a mixture of haze, sea mist and thick fog. A whole list of 'what ifs' kept rolling through his head. There had been friends and close acquaintances who had done really well. Some ended up in big time bands. Some went on to be professionals and managed to retire as early as forty. What on earth would he do now? What could he do? Indeed, what had he done with his life?

A strong maxim came into his thinking.

'Whatever I do next it ain't going to be music anymore. I've had enough.'

It seemed to come from nowhere and he wondered how such a strong thought had come to him. It kicked against all the histories of doing what was asked of him.

He downed the last dregs of warm, flat, tasteless lager and made for the light switch. The 'phone rang.

"Hello. Is that Mr. Throovest?"

The voice was familiar, but Arthur just couldn't place it.

"It's Bainsbridge-Wooley here… Rudi."

"Oh. Yes. Rudi. Yes, this is Arthur."

Before he had time to work out the meaning of a late night call from the chap who got him working in the gaol, Sir Rudi continued as if he was talking about tomorrow's weather forecast.

"I wonder if you could come and see me at Fradley on Friday night?"

Aaaaaaaaaarrrrrrrrrrgggggggghhhhhhhh!!!!!!!!

To be discontinued…

alan@pianosmith.co.uk
throovest@gmail.com